T0352127

Powerful or Powerless
in the Virtual Space

Powerful or Powerless in the Virtual Space

The Choice Is Yours!

Ghislaine Caulat

First published in 2022 by Libri Publishing

Copyright © Libri Publishing

The right of Ghislaine Caulat to be identified as the author of this work has been asserted in accordance with the Copyright, Designs and Patents Act, 1988.

ISBN 978-1-911450-95-5

A CIP catalogue record for this book is available from The British Library

Cover and design by Carnegie Book Production

Printed in the UK by Halstan

Libri Publishing
Brunel House
Volunteer Way
Faringdon
Oxfordshire
SN7 7YR

Tel: +44 (0)845 873 3837

www.libripublishing.co.uk

Endorsements

In 2017 we established a truly global leadership team and meeting regularly face-to-face became impossible. In the beginning we simply applied the rules and etiquette of our face-to-face meetings to the virtual space with limited effectiveness. We could not understand why our virtual meetings were not seen as productive or why we did not have a high level of participation. We accepted them as just a substitute for when we could not meet face-to-face ... until we met Ghislaine. She showed us how we could not only improve our virtual meetings but actually make them more effective than traditional face-to-face. This requires a paradigm shift and an awareness of new ways of working that are described in detail throughout the book. Many of the concepts described, such as "not muting" and "no cameras", are not commonly practised in most organizations and at times may feel counter-intuitive. I have personally found that implementing the insights provided has taken our virtual collaboration to a level not previously thought possible. While not easy to change culture, by following the suggestions in the book you can take the first steps to creating a high-performing and highly collaborative virtual team where everybody feels able to speak up. I strongly encourage anyone wanting to improve the effectiveness of their virtual collaboration and leadership to experiment and implement these guidelines into your way of working. As with all change initiatives, success begins with the buy-in and participation of senior leadership and they must be involved in this journey from the start.

Rob Keenan
Regional Vice President, Americas Region
Seco Tools

This book takes the reader through valuable practical cases and relatable incidents that many people will have encountered in similar ways, yet not necessarily deconstructed and evaluated alternatives. It offers an immense span of learning opportunities from hands-on experimentation and practical advice, backed up by research into building connections and associations with some of the hottest topics discussed, like DE&I, creating psychological safety and speaking up cultures, stakeholder capitalism or ethical leadership behaviours. Remote working is here to stay and growing as a competitive factor. I feel inspired and excited to experiment with counter-intuitive, unconventional settings and learn more about the opportunity for the amplification effect in the virtual space.

Sabine Weishaupt
Chapterlead, Future Leadership Design
Deutsche Telekom

As we navigate new territories of hybrid working, we must pay close attention to power in the virtual space. Ghislaine Caulat speaks with clarity and credibility on a theme that we often ignore at our peril. To really enable change and empower people we must consider well-researched theory and practice to inform our actions. In this respect, Ghislaine Caulat's book is a lighthouse in stormy seas.

Karen Dumain and Paul Taylor-Pitt
Co-leads of Do OD, the expert OD resource
UK National Health Service

Leading virtually is an inevitable mega trend, which was accelerated by the travel restriction imposed everywhere in the last two years. This book is essential for readers who are managing teams in a virtual setup. They will learn a lot from the best practices and recommendations as a guiding compass.

Rick Zhao
Head of Portfolio, Passive Safety System Division, Asia Pacific
ZF Group

A fascinating read, really challenging many of the ideas around leadership and virtual meetings, being more conscious of all the elements at play in such a setting and making them work for you to create an engaging environment. This is particularly useful if you manage across cultural and language borders, learning how to give all participants the ability to contribute. Even silence can be powerful if you learn how to use it and not fear it which so many do. I also see now why mistakes of the past were made and have an opportunity to improve the level of participation, the quality of the meetings and the output in this challenging virtual world.

Steve Plastow
Head of Sales, Industrial Trade and Converting
tesa Western Europe

Are you managing your organization or are you leading your people? Are you changing the past today, or are you transforming the present into the future? Once again Dr. Ghislaine Caulat is holding us, classically trained people, a mirror up with her groundbreaking study and work. We all have the opportunity to discover great potential among our colleagues, our peers and our superiors, if we truly collaborate on equal terms. Forget your titles and your hierarchical position for once. Start to really listen; not only to the sound but also to the content of the message. Do you really understand what is being said? Good listeners make good leaders. This book gives you great recommendations to become a real virtual leader.

Erik Uyttendaele
Head of Operations Outbound Logistics | EMEA & Intercontinental
Volvo Car Group

Powerful or Powerless in the Virtual Space – the Choice is Yours! is easy to read and understand. It is useful not only for those who work in multinational organizations – as is my case – but also because of the pandemic. It will be a great help for any executive who intuitively migrated to the virtual world and who, given that we will have to live with a new normality, will have to continue living with a hybrid labour world. Do not hesitate to rely on this book, since it has reflections and recommendations that will allow you to cultivate a more efficient and participatory virtual environment in your organization.

Luz María Aguirre
Communications and Institutional Relations Manager
AURA Observatory in Chile

This book is essential for anyone operating in the virtual space – senior leaders and organisation development professionals certainly but also anyone else who collaborates with others virtually. During the pandemic we benefited hugely from working with Ghislaine and learning how to handle doing everything online that we had previously done face-to-face. Everything Ghislaine taught us about how the virtual space is different, is here in the book, and a lot more; power dynamics and inclusion and the difference that working virtually can make, how to listen really well virtually and the importance of doing it, becoming and staying grounded and present, handling the technical aspects of online working, using one's voice well ... these are just some of the important topics covered in this book. If relationships, collaboration and authentic communication matter at all in your line of work then this book will tell you how to do them exceptionally well online!

Naja Felter
Deputy Director, Organisation Development Practice
UK Civil Service

This book was recommended to me from a practical point of view. I am a practitioner in the public education sector in Shanghai. The Omicron variant of Covid once again hit us really hard and unexpectedly in spring 2022 and the whole city is in lockdown. All school education is back to online mode once again. As a teacher specialized for the blind and a member of the leadership team of the school, I have been driving all my activities online for weeks now, from teaching the special kids in different age ranges, to organizing meetings with different teacher groups. In this special circumstance, everything is happening in the virtual space and this can be very challenging. This book is like a cure for the problem, and I couldn't help myself from echoing all the cases and examples illustrated. I strongly recommend this book to anybody leading and teaching in the virtual space.

Joyce Yin
Head of Administration Office, Head of the teaching and research group of computer science
Shanghai School for the Blind

Forced through the Covid pandemic, our organization jumped into using virtual techniques in cooperation and for leadership. Although we initially believed we performed quite well, people soon started to complain about the lack of a personal touch compared with the old face-to-face culture. As Covid continued, we started to work with Dr. Ghislaine Caulat to improve our competence in virtual cooperation. The workshops were an absolute eye-opener, delivering new, unexpected insights, that virtual meetings require very different approaches, but when applied, making them very powerful – equivalent to traditional face-to-face meetings.

This book provides an extremely valuable compilation of the methods, theories and tips to work successfully in the virtual space. It will further lead you to thinking about the (shift of) power and cooperation through virtual techniques and how to lead your business in the context of the new digital generation of co-workers. I highly recommend this book for anyone working with (locally) distributed teams, be it in a multinational or just in a modern, hybrid work-mode organization, helping to make cooperation a success in the increasingly digital workplace.

Dr. Andreas Ostrowicki
Managing Director
BGS Beta-Gamma-Service GmbH & Co. KG

Here is another great book from Ghislaine Caulat! Ever since she first introduced me to the magic of mastering virtual leadership some 15 years ago, her lessons and the results of her research have stayed with me as a foundation for virtual interaction – both as a manager in a global organization and as an internal communications professional. I have often had occasion to appreciate the lessons in how to exercise different kinds of power to influence and exercise leadership. Social-distancing measures in response to the Corona pandemic sparked unprecedented technological advancement within virtual communication, and Ghislaine's new book is a step into this new era. I recognize the book's reference to the counterproductive use of the camera in much virtual communication. I am intrigued that in her new book, Ghislaine has singled out the aspect of power. I suspect that we are witnessing a higher appreciation of knowledge and competence, which is easier to share orally via virtual means of communication. Perhaps we are beginning to apply a less exploitative and more sustainable and regenerative approach to people as another precious resource that we have to preserve and cultivate.

Hanne Ovesen
Internal Communications Manager
Alfa Laval AB

Through my experiences as a global executive manager for operations in different countries and continents, I have learned to be effective as a leader for virtual teams. It is really essential, if you are in a crisis mode or driving a significant performance change, that you have effective communication flowing from the executive management team through different levels and two-way, from leaders as well as from employees. You have to be capable of using your power as a leader to secure correct decisions as well as foster a "speak-up" culture so the decisions will be executed. All this is a balancing act, and it is sometimes very stressful to be a leader in the virtual space. This book will guide leaders on all levels with very hands-on examples of power dynamics within virtual teams. It is very important that organizations can focus on the right things in the right way such that all employees understand the importance of the decisions and execute them accurately. This is especially so in today's business climate with growing uncertainties and complexity. Thank you, Ghislaine, for your effort to understand and explain this difficult topic!

Helén Savmyr
Sensible business change leader and former SVP
Volvo Operations Bangkok

Being in a regional business role, both leading and participating in virtual meetings are very much part of my work routine. I find this book to be a very insightful and interesting read. The tips and cases shared by Dr. Ghislaine Caulat are not only useful but also open the mind to new perspectives about power in the virtual working space. I would recommend this book to anyone who is looking to get more out of their virtual working sessions.

Leong May Lin
Product Sales Manager APAC, Digital Health Solutions,
Commercial Operations
GETINGE

Contents

Acknowledgements

This book would not exist without the contribution of all twenty leaders who have been my co-researchers over more than two years. Although I mention them in their disguised identities in this book, I know that they will recognise themselves: thank you for your dedicated collaboration, trust and openness to experimentation. It has been a very enriching experience that I will always remember with gratitude!

For me virtual leadership has been a journey of on-going learning since 2003 and I would like to thank all the clients who have embarked on a virtual project with me. Thank you for your trust and the rich reflection that we have had so far and continue to have on a regular basis.

I would also like to thank Prof. Robert Thomas for his wonderful guidance through all these years of my professional career and for his encouragement for me to write a book, and not just an article, which was my original intention.

A huge thank you goes to Prof. Mike Pedler who has accompanied me in this project since the very beginning and held me to high quality standards for this research in a pragmatic and yet very effective way.

Furthermore, I would like to thank my colleagues in the Black Gazelle Team, in particular Andy Copeland for his exceptional dedication, patience and endless efforts to continuously improve the quality of the learning experience that we offer to our clients in the virtual space.

I would also like to thank wholeheartedly my colleague Elizabeth Braiden for being such a good sparring partner and for her relentless checking of consistencies, with her amazing capability of combining the helicopter view with a sharp sense for details.

Finally, I would like to thank Libri Publishing for the very good cooperation, their flexibility and commitment to quality.

Foreword

Organizations and relationships are built on conversations rather than physical infrastructures. This foundation has never been clearer since the 2020 pandemic introduced new ways of working and interacting. While virtual teams and communication have been in place for decades, the global need to support virtual connections provided more choice around the way teams gather. Ghislaine Caulat has been researching and working with virtual teams for the last two decades. I had the pleasure to meet Ghislaine in March 2021 in virtual space and immediately was engaged by the questions she was exploring about virtual teams. I have been studying communication technologies and their impact on the way organizations and individuals interact for most of my career and it was wonderful to talk with a fellow traveler on this journey!

Ghislaine's coaching work with executives, her in-depth interviews and several Collaborative Inquiry sessions with leaders around the world over a period of two and a half years form the foundation for this book, which explores the critical element of power within virtual teams. Physical, face-to-face meetings carry with them certain norms and assumptions around the communication of power that don't always translate to the virtual setting. Ghislaine provides a nuanced approach to understanding power in virtual spaces through her Action Inquiry work and her years of experience. Through this research, she provides insights and explicit recommendations for leaders who are navigating the challenges of hybrid and virtual work.

Powerful or Powerless in the Virtual Space – the Choice Is Yours questions many taken-for-granted assumptions about virtual work. For example, while many organizations are embracing the hybrid workplace to provide choice in the way people choose to attend,

Ghislaine's findings caution leaders to reflect on the power dynamics associated with this choice. Additionally, Ghislaine encourages leaders to reflect on the implications of camera use, silence, and visual and audio cues as they relate to the power dynamics created in the meeting space.

What has become clear, through her research and the global experience of changing office communication dynamics, is that leaders need to start explicit conversations about the best way to approach their meetings. Leading virtually requires a different type of facilitation. Ghislaine cautions leaders to realize that "virtual collaboration and virtual leadership belong to a different paradigm."

Early in my career, I studied telemedicine. And many healthcare practitioners would make the mistake of thinking that the doctor and patient visit was the same in teleconsultations, just occurring in a different channel. However, the change in channel had implications for the communicators' motivations, the conversation, the communicators' assumptions, and the conclusions from the visit. In the same way, the format of a meeting and the space where communicators meet have profound implications on what is said and how it is said. If our organizations and relationships are built on conversations – who gets to talk and who doesn't – then orchestrating and facilitating these conversations is one of the most critical roles of the leader.

Ghislaine's focus on power and the way it is facilitated or challenged by the virtual space helps to move the conversation around virtual meetings past the specifics of the technical platform and to examine the underlying relationships and practices that are influenced by these choices. Her focus on implications for virtual leaders in each chapter provides concrete advice and questions to consider when leading virtually. Additionally, each chapter allows the reader to focus on a different element of the process.

So, if you are new to virtual leadership, or you have experience leading in this space, or you provide guidance to these leaders, this book is a valuable resource to support your journey. By recognizing the power dynamics associated with virtual spaces, you will have more agency to orchestrate successful meetings.

Prof. Jeanine W. Turner
Georgetown University, Communication, Culture, and Technology
Program, Washington D.C. and Affiliate Faculty Member,
McDonough School of Business

CHAPTER 1 –
Why this book?

Many leaders and managers are yet to recognise that leading virtually goes far beyond having the right technology.
While increasing globalisation has been putting virtual collaboration rather tentatively in the spotlight, the COVID pandemic has made virtual collaboration unavoidable, and this almost from one day to another. What used to be seen by many as difficult and 'second-class' prior to the pandemic, suddenly became the norm and leaders found themselves catapulted into a new mode of leading and communicating. Virtual collaboration is truly nothing new and has existed for several decades, rising with the emergence of global virtual teams. Having said that, this was new for many leaders recently confronted with the need to lead and manage virtually. After a first phase of shock and an abrupt realisation that working virtually was the only way, came a phase of relief with the realisation that technology was making a lot possible: "What's the problem? We have MS Teams (or Zoom, etc.); it works!". While many of the leaders newly confronted with the need to lead virtually still believe that doing so is nothing more than leading as usual by using technology, many others – and particularly the ones who have been leading virtually for decades – have realised that technology is necessary but not sufficient. They know that leading virtually is part of a new paradigm of relating and communicating with people and requires new skills and competences alongside a different understanding of oneself as a leader.

So far, very little has been written about power in the virtual space.
In the meantime, much has been written about managing virtual teams, virtual collaboration, and virtual leadership. However, one

key aspect of virtual leadership and virtual communication in the widest sense, namely power, has not been investigated much so far. Many books have been published about power in the traditional context where leadership happens mainly face-to-face, but little has been done to understand how power shows itself (or not) in the virtual space. What Panteli and Tucker were claiming in 2009 (p. 1): "[...] though the current understanding of virtual teams has advanced in significant areas over the last few years, it has not taken sufficient account of power dynamics within virtual teams nor thought to explore the nature of power with geographically dispersed teams. [...] our understanding of computer-mediated interactions and virtual team dynamics has remained limited" is, indeed, still very valid. Furthermore, Tavenner (2019, p. 7) who wrote his doctoral thesis on a comparison of power dynamics between traditional co-located workers and remote workers claims more recently: "[...] there has been little examination of supervisor-employee interface and power relationships and, particularly, the differences that may or may not arise when supervising both co-located and remote workers."

Like Panteli, Tucker and Tavenner (pp. 5, 6), I am convinced that we need to understand better how power plays out in the virtual space, given the fact that leading and communicating in the virtual space belongs to a different paradigm, where much that is taken for granted in the face-to-face does not apply any longer in the virtual space. Let me share one key reason – among several – for that. In the context of my work with clients, I have found myself working more and more at a senior management level (Board level or Directorial level) of global organisations. Where global companies used to have a Board or Leadership Team still based in the same country (or in several countries on the same continent at most), it was still perfectly normal and relatively easy for them to meet face-to-face. However, with incremental globalisation, companies seeking to achieve some diversity at their top management levels have ended up with Boards or Leadership Teams consisting of several team members based on different continents. I have now accompanied several Boards or Executive Teams of global organisations in their virtual meetings in order to coach and help them to become high-performing virtual teams. The team dynamics (as in every other team in the face-to-face) brought to the surface clear patterns of power differentials, power plays and politics. I then started to reflect on the fact that I had coached teams for many years in the face-to-face paradigm and that, of course, power dynamics were at play then as well; what I was observing in terms of dynamics in these virtual teams was at the same time similar and different from what I knew from the face-to-face. I realised that I needed to understand more about the topic of power in the virtual space, and about its idiosyncrasies – more specifically: what is specific to power in the virtual space (if at all) and what makes it different from power in the face-to-face paradigm?

More than ever, leaders need to develop a culture of speaking up, also in the virtual space!
Given the more recent developments with the pandemic, an increasing part of organisational life happens virtually. Besides, the last years have clearly shown how important it has become for organisations to develop a culture of speaking up, particularly when something does not feel right or when wrong-doing is happening. Just to mention a few examples, such as the diesel-gate affair in 2015 (obviously there were employees at Volkswagen who knew what was going on and decided not to speak up, or if they did speak about it, their concerns were not sufficiently listened to by top management) or the 'me too' movement in society with clear impact within many organisations. There are also increasing numbers of companies which simply put diversity and inclusion at the core of their operating principles because they want to foster innovation and honour difference as a source of learning. A willingness to speak up in support of achieving this culture is likely to be a valuable resource. In this respect, in spite of the many books written about power, there are still many questions to answer about power in the face-to-face environment. As Klaas et al. mention (2012, p. 333): "It is also clear that many questions remain regarding why employees make use of different forms of voice and how managerial behaviour and organisational practices and policies might affect the actual voice within the workplace".

In a world of growing uncertainty and complexity, where organisations increasingly need to work virtually, it has become sine qua non for leaders to understand how they can helpfully display their power in the virtual space and how they can foster a climate where others can speak up and display their own power, so that organisations can thrive and focus on the right things in the right way.

CHAPTER 2 –
Who is this book for?

This book has three main target groups: leaders of virtual teams, leaders of hybrid teams as well as coaches and organisational development (OD) consultants working with virtual and/or hybrid teams. Let's look at these three target groups in more detail.

First, the book is for managers, leaders and executives in any type of organisation who lead virtual teams. This might be in a global, regional or national context. This may be in the so-called 'direct line' and/or 'dotted line', for example in matrix organisations. My experience so far has been that, while many leaders falling into this category have a sound experience of leading and managing virtually, they still have a relatively limited awareness of their power in the virtual space and on how they display it in a helpful or unhelpful way.

Second, this book is also aimed at the thousands of managers who have recently seen themselves thrown into leading so-called hybrid teams, where some employees work remotely, and other team members work from a central location or office and/or where employees work alternatively from home (remotely in the so-called 'home office' mode) and in the office. Precisely in such hybrid contexts, which are by nature deemed to create power differentials, (for example, when some employees are allowed to work from home and others not), it is paramount for a leader to understand power dynamics in the virtual space in order to lead effectively across boundaries.

Obviously, hybrid teams are not the same as virtual teams; they have similarities and additional idiosyncrasies, as I would like to show on next page:

(Global) virtual teams **idiosyncrasies**	• High levels of diversity: language, culture, background, etc. • Sometimes cross-organisational • Can be temporary or project teams • Globally or at least regionally dispersed • Often office based from different geographical locations, but increasingly also home based • Purely virtual (never meet face-to-face) or mostly virtual (meet only a very few times per year)
COMMONALITIES between (global) virtual teams and hybrid teams	• Technology mediated • Dispersed • Significant amount of work and collaboration happens virtually • Organised as TEAM
Local hybrid teams **idiosyncrasies**	• Established or permanent teams • Locally dispersed • Intra-organisational teams – with high level of identification with the company – at least before becoming hybrid • Alternate between home-based and office-based work OR • Mix of people who work home-based and others who are office-based • Mix of virtual and face-to-face collaboration

Nevertheless, because this book goes far below the surface and explores essential aspects of the virtual collaboration and virtual leadership paradigm (represented by the row 'Commonalities' in the table on page 6), I am confident that the vast majority of aspects explored in this book are also clearly applicable to the concept of power in hybrid teams and will help leaders of hybrid teams to step into their power while, at the same time, allowing their team members to do the same.

Whether you are a virtual team leader or a hybrid team leader, I would also like to underline that the book takes a shifting perspective. It looks not only at when leaders and managers are powerful in the virtual space, but it also looks at situations when leaders and managers cut other people off, for example team members or peers, from their own power: when is who powerful or powerless?

Finally, this book is also targeted at team coaches and organisational development professionals who are working virtually with virtual and/or hybrid teams and wish to widen and strengthen their expertise in virtual leadership and virtual team dynamics.

CHAPTER 3 –
What do we mean by power in this book?

Power is inherent to organisations.
First, let us recognise that while power in organisations might be seen as both positive and negative, it is everywhere and needs to be acknowledged. It is often easy to recognise when a person has power or when they have not. Bertrand Russell (1938, p. 12) was already claiming: "the fundamental concept in social science is power, in the same sense in which energy is the fundamental concept in physics". My experience is that precisely because every dynamic seems to get amplified in the virtual space, power becomes particularly visible, and it is easy to recognise when a person has power in a virtual setting. Also, power is an essential factor to determine who says what and what gets said; which statement counts as true and valid and even which action(s) result from all that. I would argue along the lines of Reitz and Higgins (2019, p. 16): "Power drives who says what to who, who gets heard and ignored. You can't escape it, it's often not fair – you have to live and work with it."

As Pfeffer (2010, p. 235) explains, "Organizational politics is everywhere. You may wish it weren't so, but it is. And because of fundamental psychology, there isn't much prospect of power and politics disappearing from organizational life."

Power is a complex and fluid concept.
In addition, it seems that the concept of power often gets associated implicitly or explicitly with other concepts, such as 'politics' and 'power'. In this case, I find the definitions offered by Buchanan and Badham (2010, p. 11) very helpful: "Power: the ability to get other people to do what you want them to do. Politics: power in action, using a range of techniques and tactics". Magee (2008) also claims

that the concept of power often gets conflated with the concepts of 'influence' or 'status' and that we should not do that. Not only is power everywhere in organisations, but it is also a rather complex concept, difficult to define in simple terms.

If you look at the numerous books and articles written about power (in general), you very soon realise that there is no homogeneous definition of what 'power' means in an organisational context. Power is sometimes seen as a 'thing' that you have or do not have. It is seen as a 'personal property' or as a 'relational property' or as an 'embedded property' – the rules and procedures that we take for granted in organisations (Buchanan and Badham, 2010, pp. 47–53). To make things even more complicated, how we see power mediates everything and the concept of power is embedded within individuals' minds (Chen et al., 2001 and Galinsky et al., 2003). As Reitz and Higgins (2019, p. 145) write: "It is more illuminating and liberating if we see power in three ways: subjective, dynamic and contextual. This allows us to see that our sense of authority changes according to circumstances […]". The questions we ask ourselves then become "when and why do I feel powerful and powerless".

As a matter of fact, it seems, as Pansardi and Bindi (2021, p. 51) claim, that the concept of power has been very dynamic and developed in many directions to date.

There is no agreed definition of 'power'.
The absence of an agreed definition of 'power' and particularly its very dynamic semantic field has led me to the following decisions for this research:

- I will not attempt to determine which definition is correct and which is not.

- I will use the framework offered by Pansardi and Bindi (2021) to make sense of and analyse the results of our research. The latter distinguish between **power-over**, **power-to** and **power-with**. 'Power-to' can also be equal to 'empowerment' or 'being able to'. 'Power-over' can also equal to 'influence' and according to Pansardi and Bindi needs to be seen as a subset of 'power-to'. 'Power-with' is defined by Pansardi and Bindi as "the ability of a group to act together in view of collective outcomes or goals".

- Together with my co-researchers, I will take a primarily relational perspective and define power as socially constructed, while not ignoring the further perspectives at the same time.

- Precisely because of the three decisions mentioned above, I will purposely NOT guide the focus of my co-researchers and will work with THEIR meaning of power. In this context, it will be essential for us to explore the questions "when do I feel powerful?", "when do I feel cut off from my power?", "when do I enable others to step into their power?" and "when do I cut off others from their power?". I will then make sense of the emerging meaning of power in the virtual space with them.

CHAPTER 4 –
Research basis for the book

Readers might find some of the contents of the book challenging, or at least counter-intuitive. In this chapter I describe the basis for my statements and the research process that I have taken so that readers can make their own judgement about the robustness of the findings. This chapter has intentionally been kept to a minimum, however more details about the research methodology and process can be found in the Appendix.

1. Collaborative Inquiry with leaders

Based on my experience of research on the topic of virtual leadership, which started in 2004, I was keen to undertake this work within the participatory paradigm (realities are co-created, also between researcher and 'researchee'), with an Action Research (see Glossary) approach. What I have learnt very clearly in my research on virtual leadership over the last fifteen years is that: if you simply interview people and ask them about leading people virtually, they often answer based on their experience of leadership in the face-to-face paradigm (often looking at what they miss virtually rather than at what they might have). In my research at that time, I found out that when people actually needed to reflect and test out new ideas, concepts and approaches in the virtual space, they would realise that they did not know what they did not know and discover new territories, opening themselves up more to new opportunities to lead well virtually.

The same approach (as opposed to an empirical approach based on online interviews, for example) seemed to be particularly necessary and relevant in order to inquire into the field of power in the virtual space, where power, as we have seen in Chapter 3, is in itself a dynamic, sensitive and delicate topic to inquire into. This is even more so when looked at within the paradigm of virtual collaboration, where many 'taken for granted' ideas seem to lose their validity and require re-examination. This point of view is clearly confirmed by researchers such as Contreras, Baykal and Abid (2020) who advocate that research on e-leadership (or virtual leadership) should be more experimental and less descriptive or empirical.

Therefore, I decided to embark on a Collaborative Inquiry (see Glossary) based on the Action Research methodology. I engaged with twenty managers from a very diverse basis in terms of cultures (there were twelve cultures, including USA, several European cultures, Middle East, Asia, i.e., China and Singapore, and Australia), in terms of organisations (corporate organisations, public organisations and NGOs) and in terms of gender (ten males and ten females). I wanted first to interview them virtually on a one-to-one basis using carefully crafted interview guidelines including questions such as "when do I feel powerful?", "when do I feel cut off from my power?", "when do I enable others to step into their power?" and "when do I cut off others from their power?", as mentioned in Chapter 3. As a result of the interviews, I was able to collect examples of times when the interviewees were either at the peak of their power or were disempowered and also times when they felt that they were enabling (empowering) or disabling (disempowering) others virtually. These examples were then described individually and presented as 'Critical Incidents' on our virtual platform (The Black Gazelle Meeting Space) so that all interviewees could read, reflect and comment on the Critical Incidents in their own time, at any moment of the process. With the terminology of Critical Incidents, I refer to Flanagan's technique (1954). Although I decided not to use the whole technique per se because this would have gone out of scope, I did decide to use the terminology of 'Critical Incident', as I felt that it was a much more accurate description than the term 'story'. The examples that I shared from the interviews all had a critical impact on the development of the virtual collaboration and/or virtual leadership described by my interviewees.

As mentioned above, the word 'power' has many different meanings, which can significantly differ from each other depending on the culture, the language or even the context in which we use it. For example, 'power' will often have a negative connotation when used in a German organisational context as opposed to an Anglo-American context, where 'power' might be seen as something more positive. For these reasons, I was very mindful of the questions that I chose to ask and how I framed them. It was important to me that the interviewees were neither guided nor constrained in their understanding of power and that they shared with me and the other interviewees what they **personally believed** 'power' was and how it gets expressed or suppressed in the virtual space. Hence, we started from a wide range of Critical Incidents related to power (there were over sixty) in an effort to let the interviewees (who I see as my co-researchers) scope with me the semantic field of power. It was for me a **Collaborative Inquiry where every voice and every meaning were equally valid**.

As represented in the diagram on next page, we went through two waves of inquiry (a wave being a complete cycle through all inquiry stages, left to right in the diagram on next page). In the first wave, I built three groups of three to four people and went through three loops of inquiry in three sessions, as described on next page. In the groups, we would explore the different Critical Incidents emerging from all interviews. At the end of the first wave, we had already identified emerging themes, which I decided to add to the basis of inquiry during the second session with wave two. At this stage, I worked with two groups, one with three and one with four members. We followed the same methodology, apart from the fact that my co-researchers were invited to reflect and work not only on their own emerging themes, but also on the emerging themes from the first wave, which made the inquiry even richer and more in-depth. More details about the research process and procedure can be read in the Appendix.

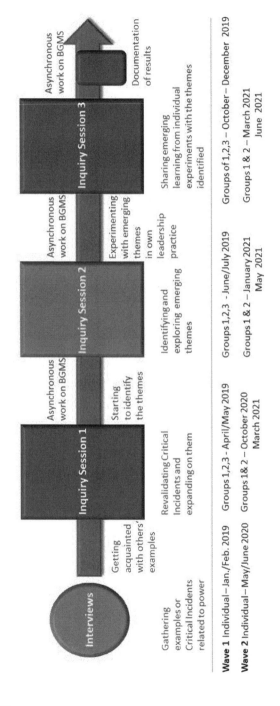

The results of these sessions will be shared in granular fashion in the chapters relating to each of the single propositions.

2. My own ongoing inquiry through 18 years of virtual leadership and virtual collaboration development

In addition to the ongoing inquiry process, where relevant, I also shared my own experience of having worked for 18 years in the area of virtual leadership and virtual collaboration development with over 2,900 managers and leaders in more than 29 global organisations. I could use the massive amount of data that I had gathered over a period of 15 years in the context of individual interviews carried out with leaders and managers from all continents across industries as well as in public organisations and NGOs.

As mentioned previously, many of the leaders that I had the opportunity to train and/or coach were executives who would invariably share with me their challenges related to power in the virtual space.

Furthermore, over the last 15 years I was also asked to coach several executive teams and facilitate virtual large group events, such as strategy conferences or innovation processes. I took this opportunity to reflect on the power dynamics unfolding in a systematic way after each of these events, together with my colleagues in the Black Gazelle team. So doing, one part of the reflection was in the form of a first-person inquiry, where I would reflect about my own role, how I stepped into my power and on the consequences this had. The second part of the reflection was a more general one about the power dynamics that we observed, their drivers and their hindrances.

3. Wider research

Finally, during the last phase of the overall process, I decided to embark on wider secondary research about the topic of power in general and the topic of psychodynamics in the virtual space, so that I could be prepared to underpin and/or question the emerging propositions from our inquiry groups with knowledge and theories from the wider field of research. I carefully decided about the timing of this step because I did not want it to influence my thinking too soon, as this might have biased the results coming from the inquiry process.

4. My co-researchers

I would like to underline that all individual names of people who contributed to this research as well as any company names have been anonymised. Great attention has been paid to making any connections to real names and companies impossible. Having said that, as mentioned earlier, they were co-researchers of twelve different cultures and more detail about each of them, including their role and where they were based can be found in the Appendix.

Furthermore, all examples taken from my own practice in virtual leadership training and coaching have been equally anonymised.

CHAPTER 5 –
How to read this book

I am presenting seven propositions in this book. My choice of the word 'proposition' is a conscious one that relies on the following two points:

1. Each 'proposition' presents an emerging theme that is robust enough to be presented in this book and nevertheless might benefit from further investigation and revalidation.

2. The word 'proposition' seems more accurate to me than 'hypothesis', because I do not only limit myself to exploring and explaining the findings, but I also look into the implications and possible approaches. As a matter of fact, all my co-researchers, who are virtual leaders themselves, were keen to explore and identify potential practical approaches and solutions. In other words, **the research was with, and from practitioners for practitioners**.

Each 'proposition' can be read independently from the others, so that busy readers can follow their interest and move flexibly through the book, instead of having to read it consecutively from the first page to the last.

In each 'proposition', the reader will find several examples of the so-called 'Critical Incidents' from the twenty leaders who contributed to the research, shared and reflected on their experience. For this reason, the text might feel anecdotal at times: I was keen to maintain the granularity of the examples because they illustrate real and concrete situations with which readers should be able to easily identify. The final chapter provides a summary of the key findings and practical recommendations for leaders and managers.

CHAPTER 6 –
Proposition 1: Mixing connection types generates power differentials

In this chapter I explain how a mix of connections (face-to-face and virtual) can create strong power differentials which affect members' 'power-to' make contributions in meetings.

Many managers and leaders often underestimate the negative impact of the following virtual meeting setting: some attendees are physically in the same room, sitting around the same table and others are linked in virtually. From now on, I will call this setting 'mix of connections'. This setting was already common before the pandemic in virtual teams because for the majority of managers, it felt unnatural to ask the people present in the office to go to separate rooms and attend the meeting separately like all attendees connected virtually. This situation has become even more common through the pandemic with hybrid teams: the team members in the office gather around the same table and the others, using their home office, join with MS Teams or similar software. This situation creates strong power differentials that usually remain unspoken, and even at times a taboo.

Team members connected virtually might feel disempowered.
Let's take one concrete example: one Critical Incident mentioned by Barbara, one of my co-researchers.

I sometimes cannot attend our Africa Board meeting face-to-face and therefore I dial-in virtually. One day, I dialled-into the meeting and others were in the same room. I tried to interject and I remember clearly what the person leading the meeting said: "yes...yes...you were not around. We have already discussed this". I shut up. I felt angry, I felt excluded, I felt chastised....like a child. I thought "you are such a knob". If I would have been in the same room, I would have said: "maybe you can update me". I would be more likely to push back and I would say: "if it is on the agenda, then there is a decision to be taken by all". In this case, I did not say anything. There is a kind of underlying feeling that people in the room think that they have made the effort to come to the place and the ones who are not should feel guilty that they have not.

This example shows how difficult it can become for people linked in virtually to hold on to their power and speak up. Whether you use cameras or not, in that situation, it was difficult for Barbara to know what the other attendees of the meeting were thinking or feeling and this added to her feeling of isolation. Were they agreeing with the leader of the meeting? Were they giving visual signals to each other as a way to comment on Barbara's contribution? The example also reveals a certain sense of culpability or guilt introjected (see Glossary – Introjection) on to Barbara. The situation led her to feel that she made less effort to join the meeting; maybe the other attendees were feeling that she was giving less importance to the meeting? However, nobody in Barbara's case, nor in many other similar cases that I have come across, would ever speak openly about these aspects; it is as if they were a taboo.

Barbara carried on with her reflections as follows:

When we have our virtual board meetings [...] I remember very well when I was 'feathered' (punished) by my own board. If I feel strongly about something, I will not step in the virtual space in front of the Board of Directors. We have this situation with a mix of connections, with people in the same physical room and people linked in to the meeting separately virtually. In the room, this is where the power is and you give up your power if you are not in the room (i.e., if you dialled in virtually). The Chairman will be in the room and will have a particular view. Others do not get included in the decision. If you are connected virtually, you cannot interject and express a different point of view. If you do, the ones in the room say: "that's what I said. Yes, you are right" even if it is a completely different point of view. There is something like a 'herd mentality'.

I would like to underline Barbara's sentence *"In the room, this is where the power is and you give up your power if you are not in the room* [but connected virtually]". This corresponds to my own experience of working with Executive Teams. Particularly when the people sitting together face-to-face in the same room are based in the Headquarters of the organisation, it makes it very difficult for individual people in the affiliates or subsidiaries of the organisation linked in virtually to actually speak up. The combination of headquarter position and sitting face-to-face while others are linked in virtually, precisely and exponentially displays power from its negative side, where people sitting away from the Headquarters and linked in virtually often feel disempowered, as Barbara describes above.

These findings are echoed in a study investigating power dynamics of four virtual global teams by Nurmi et al (2009) showing that close proximity to Headquarters increases power while isolated distant team members reported most power problems.

Team leaders connected virtually might also lose their 'power-to'.

The following Critical Incident shared by Jade shows how the mix of connections in the same meeting can also limit the leader of the meeting in their 'power-to'.

> *We had a virtual team meeting. There is the tendency for some team members to work between themselves (in smaller groups) without involving everybody. They wanted to convince me (as their leader) that this was alright. But I said: "you cannot sell this to me because we all have the right to discuss". In situations like that my voice does change. I go 'around the houses' and ask questions. The problem is that when you have people around the same table and others linked in virtually, you do not have the full picture, particularly if you yourself are linked in virtually. I feel in these cases: "this is not the right way to discuss an issue. We need to find a proper way." It is so crucial to pay attention to everything people say. Even a small side sentence can be so important.*

I find particularly the last sentence: "It is so crucial to pay attention to everything people say. Even a small side sentence can be so important," very relevant. Decision-making in diverse teams like the one led by Jade is a very delicate undertaking, where it is indeed very important to enable everybody to speak up and also to be able to hear everything that needs to be heard. The setting described by Jade does not allow this to happen and actually creates clear power differentials, which are very difficult to mitigate.

A further Critical Incident shows how even the best effort to encourage people to speak up in the virtual space in settings with a mix of connections can fail. Rose, another co-researcher, shared the following case:

> *I had to join a project which had already started. I needed to take over the lead from my manager. The project involved external partners. I was in London [on a business trip] and it had been a long day. I joined the call and three attendees were sitting in the same room. My manager mentioned that I was on the call. There were five people in total. Somebody was joining from a park and it was loud in the background. Every time when I wanted to say something, the conversation had moved on. My manager sent me a message on WhatsApp:*

"please feel free to join the conversation, if you want". I understood this as: "why don't you speak?". I actually misunderstood it. It was a genuine invitation. I did not want to intervene. I did not want to disturb. [...] If I had stepped in, we would not have reached the goal of the call. Also, the pace was very fast. There was no single moment of silence!

Rose explained how the whole setting, combined with the fact that she was new in the project, made her feel insecure and she feared that she would have 'disturbed' by asking a question. She would not own her 'power-to' and ask because of the pace of the meeting and the setting.

Mixing connection types widens the gap between team members. Another example taken from my training practice shows how the mix of connections can paradoxically widen the gap between team members in a single team. I was working with a Dutch global company, which had grown through a series of acquisitions around the globe. I was invited to work with a global team that contained members in the Netherlands, Switzerland, Japan, Singapore and the USA. The team had been working for approximately two years as a global team and was facing significant hurdles in their virtual collaboration. The team itself was composed of members from different organisations that had been acquired by the Dutch company. I started the work by interviewing every single team member individually. The problem became obvious very quickly. The four team members based in the Netherlands would sit around the same table, the three team members based in Switzerland would do the same. The two team members based in Japan would log in separately (because of the timing of the meeting, which would mean late working hours for them, so they would be working from home). The one team member in Singapore would also be logged in separately, as was the team member based in the USA, who would join the meeting from home given the time zone difference. First, the timing of the meeting was what I would call 'HQ centric'. i.e., favourable to the team members based in the Netherlands (and in Switzerland because of the same time zone) and was rather demanding of the team members based in Japan and Singapore, who had to work at night and the person based in the USA, who needed to get up very early in the morning. Therefore, this was implicitly a sign of power: not everybody was in the best conditions for work and the timing of the meeting would unfortunately not rotate according to the principle that I call 'sharing the pain'. 'Sharing the pain' would mean that the timing would be once better for Japan and Singapore, another time better for the USA and another time better for the Netherlands and Switzerland. The choice of meeting time was made implicitly, instead of openly discussing the issue and agreeing with all team members on the least painful way for everybody involved (which would have sent a clear signal that everybody's voice was equally important in the meeting). This was implicitly a statement of power, precisely because it was not made explicit and commonly agreed upon. The team members in Japan, Singapore and the USA did not consider challenging it openly but did talk about it with me in their interview.

The key aspect I would like to draw attention to in this example though is the mix of connections and the impact it had on the team performance and the work relationships. When I interviewed the Dutch team members, they would complain that the Japanese and the Singaporean team members were quiet, would never take the initiative and were not showing real commitment. They were also complaining that the Swiss team members would at times speak among themselves in Swiss German, not realising that nobody else could understand them. The Swiss team members would, on their side, complain that the Dutch team members were too loud in the meeting, making strong noises with the coffee cups drawn over the table and moving the microphone around. The Japanese team members would share how difficult it was at times for them simply to follow the conversation and to find a gap to ask a question. The Singaporean team member shared with me how awkward he felt a few times when he asked a question that was very important to him and he got no response; only a long silence followed during which he thought "Did I make myself sound ridiculous with this question?", "Did I confuse them?", etc. As a result, he decided not to speak up any longer and withdrew more from the discussions. As to the American team member, he confessed to me that he really struggled with the meetings that started at 4.00 am and that he would be very pragmatic about them. This meant that he would make sure to ask the questions that mattered to him at the start of the meeting and get the answers that he needed and would then simply listen in as a way to show presence while answering his emails in parallel, arguing that the value of the meetings was not particularly high anyway.

After having captured the different feelings and arguments, I decided to invite the whole team to an experiment as part of the training, without entering into an elaborate explanation of how the actual setting as mix of communications in these meetings was a significant part of the problem. I knew from experience that discussing it in order to change it would strengthen the high sensitivity around the topic. My experience has been that if you explain to the people gathering around the same table why they should be separate from each other to ensure 'equality' of connections, they often react in a sensitive way. They say that it is 'unnatural' or 'against common sense' to ask people to go into separate locations if they are in the same place anyway. As to the people who are logged in separately, they often feel uncomfortable about challenging the views of the co-located ones. Either because of guilt (as shown in Barbara's example above) or because of HQ centricity, where it is difficult to challenge those closer to the centre of power or even more simply out of pragmatism, thinking that the mix of communications was the most logical and natural one. Inviting them all to experiment for a limited amount of time with a setting where all are separately connected was neutralising the political and emotional aspects. Things would be reviewed after the common experience precisely based upon everybody sharing their own experience of relating differently in the team. The experiment took place and we had a thorough round of feedback, where everybody shared in a safe way what they noticed was different, how they felt in the meeting and the questions that they had as a result. After a series of three workshops, the team decided to stick to this new modus operandi and from then on, would only meet separately from each other. After a period of eight weeks, I had a follow-up with the team and they mentioned how the patterns of discussions had radically changed and how much more involved they all felt. The gaps in the team had been overcome; the team constellation had been reconfigured in a fashion where all felt that they had an equal voice with equal power.

This example shows how a simple logistical setting can generate significant gaps at a psychological level with serious impact on the team productivity because several team members find it difficult or even unsafe to speak up.

The mix of connections is particularly problematic for hybrid teams.
With the rise of hybrid teams due to the pandemic, this type of situation with a mix of connections will occur more and more, albeit on a local level, where some people will work from their home office and others from the office. Given the increased sensitivity of people in situations of mixed connections, where some team members might have the freedom to decide to work from home (at least for a certain number of days in the week) and where others might be asked to work only in the office due to the nature of their job, the difficulty linked with this setting will only grow. We may end up in situations where people working from home might decide not to enter a polemic discussion or simply not to speak up because of what they might perceive as unequal communication channels and feel disabled as a result.

Let's take the following example shared in my research:

Anna was member of a team of ten people who, before the pandemic, would work together in the same office. At the start of the pandemic, they would all suddenly work from home and find different ways of connecting and working. As the pandemic situation got easier, her company decided, like many others, to gradually allow people to work alternatively from home and from the office. The 3+2 formula (3 days home office and 2 days office) was implemented. When meetings were scheduled, the team members in the office would sit around the same table and the ones at home would log in virtually. Although the team leader made a conscious effort to involve everybody, Anna quickly noticed how difficult it was for her to make an intervention when she was logged in virtually. She would try to speak more loudly, she would also try to be strategic and wait for the 'right' pause to come in, but in most cases her point would not be taken into consideration, simply because it would not be heard. The noise around the table in the office simply made it very difficult for people outside of the room to be heard, particularly in the heated moments of discussion. As a result, Anna explained that she gave up bringing her arguments: "*I was getting tired of trying, having to speak louder and trying again; I kind of resigned, thinking that real dialogues were simply not possible in virtual meetings of that type*". As the co-researchers and I asked her why she (or any of the colleagues in the team separately connected) did not raise the issue, she said: "*Well we actually did and it was briefly discussed, but at the end of the day nothing changed apart from the resolution to pay more attention to the ones not in the room*". She then said "*and I did not want to challenge the status quo even more because I was afraid that this might bring up the underlying conflict in the team regarding the fact that some were not allowed to work from home due to the nature of their role, and others were. I was thinking to myself 'well if you have the privilege to work from home, do not rock the boat too much, even if this means that I won't be able to speak up as I was used to'*".

TO SUMMARISE

A mix of connections (face-to-face and virtual) can create strong power differentials which affect members' 'power-to' make contributions in meetings. Not only team members lose their 'power-to', but also team leaders and managers.

The main reasons for this can be summarised as follows:

- **Not being heard because of noise**: People around the same table often do not realise how much noise they produce simply by dragging papers or glasses on the table. In addition, the meeting setting does not enable all to sit at their computer in front of documents being co-created by everyone in the meeting. The sheer fact of being connected with a headset covering both ears and providing the direct contact between individuals – directly from one auditory system to the other – creates strong intimacy that is not possible with a mix of connections. As a matter of fact, the ones around the same table are in one universe and the ones connected virtually do not belong to it. It requires self-confidence, resilience and patience for the latter to stick with the discussion, stand their ground and to make sure that they are heard. The balance of share of voice as well as share of ear is disturbed.

- **Feeling unsure about others' points of view:** Most communication platforms only show on camera a limited number of attendees around the same table and their faces are often difficult to recognise, particularly if some documents are being shown at the same time. This means that the person connected virtually only receives one part of the feedback when they express a point of view. This can be disconcerting, particularly when this person asks a question and faces a wall of silence. It is no wonder that they feel unsure about the reaction of the people around the table: "Are they making funny faces about me?"

- **Feeling inferior or guilty:** As clearly shown in Barbara's example and also to some extent in Rose's example, being connected separately reinforces a certain sense of 'inferiority', where people either feel that their contribution is less valuable because they are remote or fear that their contribution is seen as less committed by the ones attending face-to-face, who might imply that the ones remotely connected are not prioritising the meeting in question to attend it face-to-face. As explained earlier, the main difficulty is that all these feelings, assumptions and interpretations remain most of the time in the implicit and develop into a taboo, disabling the ones connected virtually from stepping into their 'power-to'. My experience is that this happens even with the best facilitators trying to mitigate the power differentials through attentive and precise facilitation.

- **Symbolic centre of power:** People sitting together around the same physical table usually have more power. Not only because of the fact that they have more channels of connection (face-to-face with eye contact, body language, etc.) but also because of the actual place where they meet, especially if this happens to be the Headquarters of the organisation in question.

IMPLICATIONS FOR VIRTUAL LEADERS

If leaders want to avoid strong power differentials in their teams, they need to avoid meetings based on a mix of connections with some people located in the same physical place and others linked in virtually, where and whenever they can.

I very often get confronted with the following arguments from virtual leaders:

1. "It is so unnatural to ask the team members who are in the office to go to separate places to attend the meeting. They are so happy that they can finally be together again physically!". I am actually not sure that this is so unnatural; it might be counter-intuitive at first glance. It might take some effort from virtual leaders to explain to their team members why the need to have everybody connected in the same way is so important, but it is certainly worth it. If these habits do not get challenged, then implicit power dynamics will become more and more established, and it will be very difficult to challenge them in the long run.

2. "We cannot have people in different places while in the office. We do not have enough separate offices!". Particularly companies with so-called open plan offices find it difficult to establish a virtual meeting culture where everybody is connected separately. Here I can share the following tips that have been implemented by many of our clients:

   a. You can install some discrete individual zones within the actual open plan office, for example in the form of meeting 'boxes' which are sound insulated and equipped with the necessary logistics for prompt plug-in. One of our clients calls these spaces 'cockpits'. Another option is to have dedicated corners adequately separated with plants or any other device where people can go and attend their virtual meeting.

   b. You can equip your team members with high-quality noise-cancelling headsets, which will allow them to attend their virtual meetings from their respective desks. It is important that the headsets cover both ears because this will allow them to become immersed in the virtual space and the meeting that they have joined, almost forgetting what is going on around them in their physical environment.

c.   You can encourage your team members to work as much as possible from their home office when they meet virtually with colleagues.

CHAPTER 7 –
Proposition 2: No camera for more power!

In this chapter I illustrate how the absence of visuals in the virtual space can be significantly empowering. By not using cameras, leaders and team members will increase their chance of speaking up about what really matters to them, and step into their power. This however requires specific important skills.

The importance of seeing people in virtual meetings has been overstated.

Many managers and leaders think that they need to have their camera switched on in order to see how their message lands with people. They believe that they can know that from body language. They also believe that by seeing people on camera, they can check whether people are indeed listening to them or actually doing something else (e.g., writing emails or chatting to colleagues). Most technology is still suboptimal in terms of showing everybody's face; for example, if you are sharing a document and have more than eight people attending your meeting on MS Teams (these are six on WebEx and Adobe Connect and four on Zoom – see all technical details in Appendix 4), you might end up not seeing the rest of the meeting attendees. Furthermore, cameras require a higher bandwidth and therefore, depending on the location of meeting attendees, not everybody can have their camera on, which in itself creates interesting power dynamics, particularly when no rule about the use of camera has been agreed on in the team. In addition, I would argue that even when face-to-face we like to believe that people are listening to us when they look at us and put on an interested face. My question to you, the reader, here is (please, be honest with yourself): How many times have you been watching a person in a meeting or in a public speech, looking focused on what they say, but actually with your mind wandering miles away with thousands of questions, such as "When will this monologue end?" "Will I manage to get my shopping done tonight?" etc. We like to believe that we can control people if we see them, but actually we can't and the virtual space makes this very clear to us. Instead of exercising power through control of cameras (which would be based on a sender-focus of communication), I would argue that the virtual space should be receiver-focused and the sender's responsibility is to make his/her message compelling and engaging in its content as well as in its delivery, so that s/he can attract attention.

When feeling strongly about something, not seeing others' faces makes you more fearless.

The inquiry with my co-researchers brought to light that actually the absence of visuals in the virtual space can be significantly empowering. Let's have a look at the following Critical Incident shared by co-researcher Steve.

> *We were in an HR country-council meeting. We were going through a centralization process and everybody was having to re-apply for their job. In three seconds, I took the decision to speak up, and said that I was not going to re-apply, even if it meant that I would lose my job. I argued that the interviews would bring no new information after 10 years of experience. I said that such a procedure was not suitable for a performance-based company. My boss, Claudia asked me why I felt that way. I answered that if we are a performance-driven company, then we should acknowledge performance and that the interviews would be a sham, just a hollow exercise. My boss said that she would take my concern to her own boss, even if she did not agree with me. After the meeting, I got a tremendous reaction from my colleagues attending the meeting. They did not speak up during the meeting because they were worried about losing their jobs. In their view what I did was high risk, but I was fearless. I really felt that I needed to step up because I would have been 'less myself' if I just accepted the interviews, as this procedure went against my values. It was as if these interviews were something that was pushing against one of my drivers. Actually, I was scared, tingly, but I felt that it was all crap. In asking why I felt that way, Claudia's professionalism gave me the courage to continue speaking.*

Afterwards, I questioned the whole experience. I felt alone and feared that everybody might have felt that I was the issue. I did not really regret it though: it was such a strong feeling, so deep inside.

We explored in the group what made Steve so fearless; he shared that precisely because he did not see the faces of his peers (they were all connected virtually with no camera on), he was more in touch with himself, with his own values and with the topic of the discussion. He was not distracted by the facial expressions of his colleagues and was not seeking their approval. He was simply himself, genuinely sharing what he was thinking and feeling in the moment. It felt like walking on the edge for him (he was 'scared') but he felt driven by a strong sense of authenticity and the need to speak up.

Let's take a further Critical Incident from Rose:

I am usually very careful. I do not speak up that much. Most of my meetings now happen virtually. In my previous company, we did not have many virtual meetings. Last week I was asked to join a focus group. It was about an engagement survey. Usually, this type of meeting was rather top-down, and we were more in a listening mode. This time we had no slides, no agenda. I offered to share my thoughts and others followed me. I wanted to break this awkward silence. I felt that I did not have any choice. If I did not speak, nobody would. I thought: "For once, we are being given the chance to express ourselves!". I thought: "If we don't speak now, we never will do!" I also felt a bit competitive. I did not want to be part of the silent group. Once I started to speak, others followed me. They were saying: "as Rose said, etc.". If the meeting would have been face-to-face, I would probably not have spoken up. I would have felt more emotional and hesitative. I feel more comfortable when behind the screen or at the phone. My emotions are hidden. I can express myself better on the phone.

This example also shows that Rose, like Steve, was more focused on herself and her thoughts through the absence of visual clues and she was therefore less fearful to move forward and speak up. She was not distracted by the other meeting attendees and could carry on with the same level of focus. In the same way that she could not see others and therefore interpret their emotions, she also felt protected because she could not be seen either, which gave her a stronger sense of control and allowed her to be more assertive.

A further Critical Incident shared by Steve also describes very well this feeling of fearlessness and stronger focus on one's own thoughts:

It was in one of our regular project meetings when we were trying to rebuild a tool kit. One person from Sweden, one from APAC, one French guy based in Germany, one Portuguese (and me as American) were meeting virtually to put the tool kit together. We had a series of meetings and I remember one of them particularly well. They had used the tool before in other countries and were suggesting how we could use it in the US. They were intending to solve every single problem and I had a strong sense that what they were describing was going to become very complex. I was pretty sure that we would not have a good product at the end of it. I could fully understand in which direction they wanted to go. I began to ask questions. I was trying to get them to realise that there was another good perspective. Not only was I asking the questions, but I was also providing examples of how I would see it developing and giving them the assurance: "I get what you are saying". It felt really important to me to explore concrete measures. I also challenged them by pointing out that, if we had solutions working, why would we change them? In the end, we concluded that they were right for their situation, and I was right for my situation (in the US). It was not 'one size fits it all': there were some nuances needed. They were all professional and sensible people and they understood things from my perspective. I had managed to turn the meeting around: from "the solution is there, and you just need to implement it in the US" to "we need to be pragmatic and allow some variations".

If I had looked at these people face-to-face, I feel that this would have limited me. Actually, the fact that I could not see their body language gave me the courage to push my view in an assertive way. I practiced the virtual nods [mmhm, yeah, etc.] and open questions ("what are you thinking?"). Also, the fact that nobody was on mute and that we took the time to introduce ourselves in a personal way at the start helped a lot to set the right atmosphere.

You need to put a few conditions in place to foster fearlessness.
In my view, the last sentences describing Steve's situation are very important. The absence of visual clues in a virtual environment can clearly be empowering (strengthening the 'power-to'), provided that some important factors are in place. One key factor is taking the time at the start of a meeting to establish what I would call 'the human connection' and allowing everybody's voice into the virtual space so that everybody can connect emotionally with each other. A process to achieve that can include for example asking a simple question such as "What would make a successful meeting for me today?" and inviting all the meeting attendees to answer this question. This allows people to get into the flow of the conversation without losing their own sense of themselves. Two other important aspects are the fact that Steve was paying attention to asking open questions and nodding virtually: these were two connection channels which, in the virtual space, are much more effective than seeing body language.

Finally, in my view, Steve practised an essential aspect, which is to make sure that everybody is unmuted so that spontaneity and intimacy can develop in the virtual space. The tragedy is that the traditional digital etiquette requires that people remain muted until they speak or are asked to speak, which is in itself a strong disabling intervention technically and literally cutting people off from their voice. I always challenge my clients about this rule, because in my view this is the most counter-productive one you can think of! It generates a controlled environment, with stilted conversations where people are asked to raise their hand (using the corresponding symbol on the platform) if they want to speak and are then granted the 'right' to speak (or not) and unmute themselves. This practice does not allow any dialogue, in the best case a ping-pong debate! When I introduce the rule of 'not muting', to my clients, I often get the reaction: "But this is going to be really loud and chaotic!" Obviously, if people are not asked beforehand to be in a quiet space, then this will probably happen. Doing some clear 'contracting' about key rules upfront of a meeting (for example in this case, agreeing beforehand about the necessary logistics and behaviours) is essential. Paradoxically and very interestingly, I would argue that the more leaders or facilitators of meetings – or virtual events of any type – ask people to mute so that it might give them a sense of control of their environment with no disruption, the more they might actually lose power in the sense of 'power-to' connect and reach people. When people are muted, they feel freer to disconnect or do something else while attending the meeting and might pretend that they attend, while actually attending to other activities.

In the flow or in the grip?
While the absence of visuals can certainly empower people and increase the probability that they speak up and voice their point of view, even if the latter is not in agreement with the rest, there is in my experience a very important difference to be made. I would like to call this difference: 'being in the flow' as opposed to 'being in the grip'. 'Being in the flow' means that, particularly in my role as leader or meeting facilitator, I connect with all attendees at a deeper level. For example, by paying attention to what is being said and what is not being said as well as how it is being said, paying attention to people's tone and silences, paying attention to the rhythm of the conversation (is it fluid or rather staccato?), etc. This requires a real effort to open up oneself and let the flow of the conversation carry you, without losing the sense of yourself (otherwise you would collude with the rest of the group). 'Being in the grip' means, on the other hand, being fearless and not letting oneself be influenced by others and standing one's own ground, but potentially responding from a place of high sensitivity when somebody might have said something that leads you to some irrational or emotional reaction, independent of the actual topic of the dialogue. In other words, 'being in the grip' means getting 'one's own buttons pressed' and becoming self-referential in one's own reactions. I have learnt that the virtual space actually increases the probability of getting in the grip, if one is not well grounded in one's own self-awareness (see Glossary) and does not attend the meeting from a place of robust mindfulness. This in turn requires some practice such as what we call a 'focus exercise' (see an example of a focus exercise referred to in 15.3 in the Appendix) to be carried out either individually before the meeting in question or in the meeting (depending on the level of mindfulness maturity of the group of attendees).

Let's start with examples of 'being in the flow' and let's explore how these situations give you a strong power (in the meaning of 'power-to' and 'power-with').

Sarah goes with the flow.

During one of our sessions, Sarah shared the following situation:

She was leading a meeting with a team that she had known for a long time, and they were working on a big change programme. Although the company's culture was usually very action orientated, on that day, the team told Sarah not to move on too quickly with the agenda. They stuck with slide two of the presentation and a whole rich and wonderful discussion unfolded. At that moment it felt risky to Sarah to let go of the agenda, but she received very positive feedback afterwards. She shared how she experienced the power that one might feel in the moment of letting go of the agenda and going with the flow.

We looked at how – paradoxically – letting go (of the agenda) and going with the flow (i.e., giving power to others in the meeting) might give you even more power in the end. I shared how I also experience this regularly in my virtual workshops and how I often feel that I am walking on the edge, constantly going with the flow and thinking at the same time "Is this still the right thing to do?" There is something really powerful in this aspect. We went on and explored questions such as: What is the part that confidence plays in that? And the role of preparation? As well as clarity of roles and clarity about boundaries? My experience is that preparation certainly plays a big role: the better I am prepared, the more I am ready to throw the agenda out of the window and go with the flow. We finally asked ourselves: how is that different from face-to-face? Sarah asked herself: "If I had been face-to-face, would I have thrown the agenda out of the window more quickly?" After some further exploration and reflection, the whole group of five (four co-researchers and myself) came to the following conclusion:

In a virtual context, people are not afraid of losing face if no camera is used because they are more in contact with themselves and their intuition and might therefore more often be 'walking on the edge'. Our experience is that we can indeed better go with the flow virtually if no camera is used, because we can concentrate much more on the flow of the conversation and we recognise the 'music' unfolding. With cameras, the facial expressions distract us, the audio connection becomes less impactful, and we disconnect from the flow of the exchange.

If I had overthought about the situation, I would have lost the flow!

Let's have a look at a further situation shared by Lynn, another co-researcher.

> *I lead a local network of 12 people and I have been working with them for three or four years. The network deals with a tough and big change process, which requires strong collaboration and the willingness to deal with the mess. It can be very difficult at times to reach an agreement. During our last virtual meeting, we had a proper check-in at the start and I felt that we needed to put the group dynamics in the focus and to prioritise them. I was simply allowing the important conversations to happen; I was asking the right questions and containing the anxiety.*
>
> *At the end of the meeting, I got the feedback from the attendees that the meeting was very valuable.*
>
> *During the meeting, I was feeling calm. I felt very focused and in the moment. I felt that I was being in the flow. If I had overthought the situation, I would have lost the flow! I was picking up the cues as we were going through the conversation and I was changing the agenda in the moment, continually checking back and I was making sure that everybody had a voice.*

Here, I would like to draw particular attention to the statement "If I had overthought the situation, I would have lost the flow!" This also corresponds to my own experience: as everything gets amplified virtually, there is real potential for getting into the flow of thoughts and emotions much more quickly than in face-to-face. It is important to ride the flow lightly, without – as Lynn explains – *"'overthinking' too much and holding too tightly to the original plan AND, at the same time, without letting oneself be completely overtaken by the flow and losing the sense of purpose and direction for the meeting".* This represents a real skill in leading virtual meetings that can provide real 'power' in the sense of 'power-to' and 'power-with'.

The following Critical Incident shared by Marcus, a further co-researcher, also displays a wonderful case of 'power-to' and 'power-with' through going with the flow at an emotional level:

> I was leading a call with several people in supply management. People were calling in from Poland, Germany, and other European countries. I could hear the difficulties that they were encountering very clearly, and I therefore decided to share my feelings about that with them. This connected me immediately in a very strong way with them. They really felt that I was with them. Whenever I suggested something, they would follow with high attention, and we could move forward looking at different processes and how we could amend them.

The above situation clearly shows the impact of being able to really connect at an emotional level in the virtual space. I would argue that this paradoxically might be easier if one connects without camera, because one has a stronger focus on what is being said and on the music of the conversation. This is particularly true if one uses a headset covering both ears, because this enables direct communication from one nervous auditory system to the other nervous auditory system. I would also claim that Marcus was experiencing 'power-to' as he was able to help everybody overcome the barriers that they were encountering and to galvanise their efforts to focus on the necessary measures to take and to agree on them. He was also experiencing 'power-with' because by galvanising everybody's energy, they were *together* able to look at the different processes to amend them.

Based on my own experience, I completely agree with the above. The example shows how connecting strongly at the emotional level, particularly in the virtual space, can lead to a strong sense of 'power' or 'empowerment' (power-to). I know that I feel 'powerful' every time I manage to go fully with the emotional flow of the participants' energy and to leave my design/plan behind – at least for a little while. This 'ride' of going with the flow virtually is, for me, usually much more intense than face-to-face and I more often get the feeling of walking on the edge virtually. Paradoxically, this is when most changes happen on the participants' side.

Headset-to-headset connection is your entry ticket for emotional connection.

At this stage, I would like to build on several of the comments made earlier and underline that virtually, it is easier to go more quickly with the flow of the conversation in a meeting precisely because of the strong audio-connection enabled through headsets covering both ears and establishing (thereby) a direct line between the auditory nervous systems of the sender and recipient. If no camera is used, this connection can become very impactful and strong. If cameras are switched on, then the strength of the audio connection becomes diluted, because people's attention is divided between the picture of themselves on the screen, the pictures of other attendees on the cameras and some documents shared at the same time. Holding the attention in that way can be very tiring and therefore the concept of 'Zoom fatigue' emerges. The point is obviously not about a specific virtual collaboration technology but about this habit of using cameras at all costs, whether this is on Zoom, Skype, WebEx, Adobe Connect, MS Teams, etc. it does not make any difference. What does make a difference is that people have to focus very hard on themselves (how do I look on the camera?) and on other people's eyes (people feel that they need to have permanent eye contact online). As Leighton (2021) describes in her analysis of four causes for 'Zoom fatigue', in a face-to-face meeting people would not watch themselves in the mirror all the time, nor stare at other people all the time. No wonder they get tired. Under such circumstances, people will not be able to 'go with the flow'.

The above situations are clear examples of 'being in the flow' and therefore finding the 'power-to'. Let's have a look now at some examples that might hint at 'being in the grip'.

When John, Barbara, Jeff and Steve were in the grip.

John, another co-researcher, shared the following Critical Incident:

> *We had a virtual meeting in my team [a team with 14 managers from various European countries]. At some point, the conversation started to turn into a general moaning circle: the world is bad, this is their fault, etc.*

> *I was thinking: "All these stories are old stories. It feels like being in kindergarten. My goodness you are all senior managers!" I was feeling*

angry, unnerved, somehow disappointed by the discrepancy between what these managers at their level should be doing and how they were actually behaving.

I said: "We are now stopping this discussion. This does not lead us anywhere". I said it with a strong voice. My sense is that people knew that I was serious.

After my statement, everybody kept quiet. It seems that nobody saw that coming. Then, after a while, the conversation moved on to another topic. I did not receive any feedback from anybody after that meeting. I was wondering if maybe some people thought: "This is unbelievable! How could he do that!"; maybe others were thinking: "Thank God he intervened!". After the meeting, I had a moment of doubt: was it the right thing to do (to intervene that way)? Then I thought: "So what?" In my view they were crossing the line and therefore that was the right thing to do.

John's doubts seem to be justified here; we (the three co-researchers and myself) explored these in depth at the inquiry session. The key question was: was John reacting this way because he got caught in his own sensitivity and emotions? In other words: were some of his buttons being pushed? There was indeed something judgmental in John's reaction, which was mainly emotional (he was feeling "angry, unnerved, somehow disappointed"). This is an indication that he was 'in the grip', which led him to the abrupt intervention. In this situation, intervening without 'being in the grip' might have looked like: "I notice that we are going in circles and stuck on negative thoughts. What is happening right now? … How do we want to deal with these emotions?" Confronting the team in that way might have opened the door to explore the team dynamics at a deeper level and to help the team move forward. The interesting question here is: who had 'power-over' whom? Who lost the 'power-to'? You could argue that John, because of his hierarchical position as leader of this executive team, had the 'power-over' the rest of the team and the discussion was stopped. He also had the 'power-to' stop the discussion via his abrupt intervention. However, one could argue that he might have lost some of his 'power-to' in the mid-term, as his team members withdrew from the conversation and did not communicate with him any further after the meeting. This means that John had to work afterwards (as he mentioned in the inquiry session) to re-establish the relationship and reconnect with everybody so that he could recover his 'power-to' in further discussions. Withdrawing and 'hiding' in the virtual space is much easier than face-to-face. Hence in this case, paradoxically, the team members might have had more 'power-to' than they might have thought in the first place.

Let's have a look at a further situation describing 'being in the grip'. Barbara describes the following case:

We had a virtual meeting and the director in India kept meandering. I must have felt irritated on that day. I said: "BJ, while we all like to listen to your stories, maybe we ought to go back to the agenda". Basically, I told him to shut up. I thought that my tone was a bit brutal. Then a silence followed. Everybody got silent. At the end of the meeting, I felt awkward. Usually, I think that I am culturally sensitive. This time I was not. I was simply too irritated. If we would have had the meeting face-to-face, I would still have intervened. Maybe my tone would have been different. I do feel safer in the virtual space, however I am not a meeting troll. If you cannot see the people, there is nothing to restrain you. The social walls are different.

When we explored this Critical Incident at the inquiry session, Jeff concluded:

Lots of people think at the beginning that operating in a virtual environment is limiting their impact on others. Many comments [in our work here] seem, in fact, to indicate the contrary!.

Jeff himself shared the following Critical Incident:

We had a virtual meeting that I was leading. An argument started to emerge between two of the attendees; it was a meeting that they were planning to attend independently of each other, with one of them getting frustrated about that. It was clearly an issue between the two of them. We had time pressure and I felt that I had to cut it short. I said: "This is not a topic for discussion". The sound of my voice and my tone were harsh. The words that I used were OK, but I lost my temper. It was not typical for me. I tried to correct this mistake by asking the main protagonist of the argument a further question, encouraging him to say more about what he did. He actually apologised. He said that he would take the topic with his colleague offline. He backed off. He became quiet. I thought: "He is gone for the rest of the meeting". After the incident, there was a dead silence. All were shocked. I felt that it was a lost opportunity. I did not get all of these people together very often. In that moment, I felt bad for everybody. I tried to ask questions to the rest of the group in order to 'recover' and it took me twenty minutes to get things back on track again.

In the two cases above, it seems that Barbara as well as Jeff quickly became aware that they were 'in the grip'; nevertheless, it was too late, and the impact had already taken place. They had both disempowered the meeting attendees in question. Both examples show how difficult it was to recover from the incidents, again precisely because everything gets amplified in the virtual space. We discussed both Critical Incidents at the following inquiry session and Jeff reflected: *"To me this is another example where the virtual situation is multiplying the impact of what we say with much more strength than we wanted. A delicate tool to use correctly."* To which Steve replied: *"I agree Jeff. But I also feel it is something you can put on the table, the fact that things may seem more intense because we only have our voice, so we all have to adjust a bit and not let things bother us or ask if someone is upset, because it sounds that way".* Steve underlines here a very important competence of virtual leaders, one connected with deep self-awareness (see Glossary) that enables them to discern quickly whether one is 'in the grip', as opposed to 'in the flow' and to bring what is happening into the open, which might mean showing one's own weakness of communication in the specific instance, which would in turn empower (in the sense of giving 'power-to') the team members to recover their voice and speak up again.

Let's now have a look at a further case from Steve, which in my view raises an additional important question, namely how do you stop unhelpful behaviour in a team without disempowering everybody?

We are in a virtual strategy meeting in my team. C. was one team member, and he was so different from the rest of us. He is a difficult person to work with. Every twenty minutes, he was bringing the same idea again. I said: "C. from your perspective, I see why you would say that, but we need to move on!" I thought silently: "You keep dragging us back. You need to have your head open!" I totally shut him down! I felt absolute frustration with him. I had all that baggage by seeing him as a 'difficult person to work with'. I regretted having shut him down. If we would have been face-to-face, we would have talked over each other. We would have moved on through that. Virtually, we leave the space to the person to speak up. As a result, I had to cut him off sharply. After the meeting, C. came to me and said that he felt shut down. During the meeting nobody said anything. We simply moved on. C. must have felt very alone. I also think that I slowed down the meeting with this intervention, because I could feel how the energy of the team went down.

I would like to underline one specific reflection shared by Steve: *"If we would have been face-to-face, we would have talked over each other. We would have moved on through that. Virtually, we leave the space to the person to speak up. As a result, I had to cut him off sharply."* This aspect resonates strongly with me. Face-to-face (or even in a setting with cameras on), the attention might have been less focused on the person and their arguments because of the visual distractors such as people watching other people's movements, or what is happening in the background, etc. In an audio environment with cameras off, people's attention was more focused on the person called C.; therefore C. became more figural and potentially more present to all. The fact that Steve and C. did not speak over each other is probably due to the digital etiquette of not interrupting people before they have finished speaking, as a sign of respect, which paradoxically let Steve cut C. sharply with a tone and in a fashion that were not respectful. In addition, Steve was also 'in the grip': *"I felt absolute frustration with him. I had all that baggage by seeing him as a 'difficult person to work with'".* In this case, the situation again required heightened self-awareness so that Steve could recognise what was happening to him in the moment and potentially correct the course of action through a different intervention.

Interrupting people helps to remain in the flow.
Steve's situation described above also required the use of a different digital etiquette, which is to interrupt people (see also page 118). Over the years, I have learnt that the traditional teleconferencing

etiquette, which then became a digital etiquette and entails rules such as: "Do not interrupt people and wait until they have finished speaking, go on mute if you have nothing to say and mention your name before you speak" actually lead to very unproductive communication patterns in the virtual space. The meetings feel sterile or at least stilted and there is no space for a natural dialogue to develop. On the contrary, this type of etiquette contributes to developing a virtual meeting culture focused on the 'sender'. It strengthens advocacy patterns and at best 'ping pong' arguments (i.e., "I think that ..." – "No, I think this is wrong and here is what I think", etc.). The fact that Steve felt he needed to let C. finish what he had to say actually amplified the spotlight on C. and his repetitions felt even heavier. As an alternative, if Steve had joined the flow of the conversation and interrupted C., he might have been able to enter into a 'dance', holding the arguments lightly in a pacing and leading fashion and enabling the conversation to move on.

At this stage, it is really interesting to notice what Pfeffer (2010, p. 140) writes about interrupting in relation with power in general: "One source of power in every interaction is interruption. Those with power interrupt, those with less power get interrupted. In conversation, interrupting others, although not polite, can indicate power and be an effective power move, something noted by scholars in a field called conversation analysis. Men interrupt others more frequently than women, and doctors seldom listen to their patients for very long without interrupting. In each instance, patterns of conversation reinforce differences in power and status derived from other sources such as general social expectations and expert authority." I would argue that the traditional digital etiquette has embedded these implicit power patterns in virtual collaboration, based on what people experience face-to-face. In order to create a virtual collaboration culture in which people speak up and enter a genuine dialogue, it is essential to go against these patterns and to encourage everybody to interrupt each other, independently of what their status might be. Now it is even more interesting to notice how, unfortunately, specific features on many virtual collaboration platforms actually cement these implicit embedded power patterns. Many leaders or facilitators of meetings or workshops ask people to click on the 'raise hand' button if they want to speak up. In my view, this is a clear example of where virtual collaboration technology can be paradoxically destructive to collaboration and genuine dialogue by manufacturing rituals. It is about time that people became highly critical and started understanding the embedded power systems in virtual collaboration software, in order to make a conscious decision on which features to use or not to use. I will come back to this important aspect in Chapter 8. For now, I will simply reiterate the urgent need to encourage people to interrupt.

Process awareness˙ is essential to maintaining one's own 'power-to'.
The above case from Steve resonated very strongly with the vast majority of co-researchers involved in this project. Most of them stated that they were facing the same challenge. During a subsequent inquiry session, we explored this incident further. Steve shared the following:

> I am still bothered by it. I am not the manager of this individual. Face-to-face, people would have challenged him through body language. I said something and it did shut him down. [...] I felt that I had to stop it. However, I cannot accept this feeling that you sacrifice the one for the rest.

Jeff said what he would do in similar situations: *"I tend to play the 'idiot'. I say something like: 'I want to be sure that I understood your point' and then I summarise it. When the person repeats the point again, I intervene along the following lines: 'I am lost because this is what you said a few minutes ago ... or am I missing something here?'"*

Jeff went on, adding to what I believe is an essential point: *"Some people behave like that because they feel very insecure. I have this pattern in the meetings with my Board".*

Indeed, the aspect of uncertainty plays a very big role in these instances; I often have such behaviours in my workshops. I try to be appreciative of what can be truly appreciated in what the person says, so that they feel recognised and *seen* in the virtual space; then they can relax and feel less unsure as a result. Paradoxically it seems that the need to be seen and acknowledged in the virtual space is, for many people, much stronger than face-to-face.

---

*   See Glossary

We then explored how we can combine the 'challenging' with the 'appreciative'. In this context, we mentioned that it was not about appreciating something said that was not helpful. It was more a question of finding something in what was said that could be appreciated as a way to calm the person down. We discussed in this context the difference between working on the process (of psychodynamics) and less at the content level with such a person.

This incident makes a further competence clear when it comes to exercising positively one's own power in such a way that enables others to step into their power, instead of shutting them down: this competence is process awareness. In this case, Steve might have focused on the process and much less on the content for a little while by recognising C.'s need to be *seen* or acknowledged so that the latter could relax and the conversation could have moved on.

Giving feedback in the virtual space will be sharper than face-to-face and can significantly increase the 'power-to' if done skilfully.
Let's now open the scope of our reflection a bit further and concentrate on giving feedback to an individual during a virtual meeting without shutting him/her up and in a way that is – in fact – empowering. This question raised a very lively debate in one of our inquiry groups.

John shared the following situation:

One of my team members was again speaking in one of his usual monologues. He was speaking about things that were discussed a long time ago and that we had also discussed many times. I said "S., this is enough. We have already heard these issues. I have the feeling that you speak only for the sake of speaking, but this does not lead to any solution". Very shortly after I said that I thought: "You idiot!" (towards myself). S. was completely silent. After a few seconds, I thought: "This is what it is, I cannot excuse everything!" Then I even felt wonderfully well, and I was thinking: "The team needs to notice that this kind of behaviour is not acceptable." Afterwards, I wondered: "Have I let myself be provoked? Should I have been more diplomatic? No, you need to be authentic!" Maybe if I had been less spontaneous, would I have chosen my words better? On the other hand, if I had tried to be more diplomatic, I might have lost some of my authenticity and appeared like a 'softy'?"

I called S. a few days later and asked him whether he understood my reaction. I explained to him that I simply could not accept such a behaviour and he seemed to understand. We did not discuss this any further in the whole team. Having said that, one time, as S. was falling into the same patterns again, one of the colleagues said to him: "S. simply let it be, please stop." It seemed that in this moment the team started to display a behaviour that I had been modeling with my authenticity.

In my view, with this Critical Incident, John again points out another very important aspect: remaining authentic without shutting anybody up, while giving feedback to that person. I would argue that this situation also illustrates 'being in the grip' and that the aspects explored before apply to this case as well. Hence, I would claim that there is a fine line between 'being authentic' and 'shutting people up' and that this fine line is about having the right skills to offer feedback in an authentic way, as much as possible detached from one's own emotions and more focused on the receiver of the feedback. I completely agree with John that, in this instance, it was necessary to stop the behaviour in question and that the fact that this was done (not how it was done) had a positive impact on the team, enabling S.'s colleagues to take ownership of the process and challenge S. as well. Now, for most of my co-researchers, the question became: can we/ should we offer feedback to an individual in public, in other words, during a virtual meeting where other colleagues attend?

Jeff shared the following very interesting incident:

I was leading a virtual meeting which was getting quite rough. People were trying to define their point of view, but they were getting aggressive, also at a personal level. At one point, I addressed one person who got very aggressive, and I said: "Personal attacks are not acceptable!" The person shut up and remained quiet for the rest of the meeting. Others were also quiet. It was as if they were also feeling responsible for what happened. I could feel that everybody was tense and thinking intensively about what they could say next. I was feeling full of regret. I was sorry to have become angry like that. I was not proud of myself. I actually did not regret having intervened, but I was regretting my tone and my anger. It was a very difficult group, which was turning in circles. I had to escalate the issue to my boss, who then spoke on a one-to-one basis to the main person who was blocking the discussion.

Steve had the following reaction: "*That's a tough situation for sure. I am wondering though, is it ok when people are feeling awkward after a situation like that to say something like – 'Does anyone else feel "funny" right now? What can we do to get back on track?'* "

In this situation, I would agree with Steve and argue that one big opportunity was lost for this group, namely, to reflect on their aggressiveness and the way they were communicating with each other. Jeff confronted one of them, but actually many of them were displaying the same behaviours. Here it seems that Jeff was not 'in the grip' and that he was simply playing his role as leader and guardian of professional communication, even if he was not satisfied with the way he did it. I wonder what would have happened if Jeff had intervened along the following lines: "I observe the aggressiveness that we are playing out today in the group. I also think that some of this aggressive communication is not acceptable and that we ought to stop it immediately. What do you think is actually happening?" This obviously might have been a difficult conversation, but it may have helped the group to grow by reflecting about their dynamics at a deeper level. Jeff decided to take the issue on an individual basis, certainly for good reasons. What was achieved was that the group became aware of unacceptable behaviour, but the danger in this approach is that they might have detached themselves from this behaviour by focusing only on the person called out by Jeff.

The debate on giving feedback individually or in the group went on among my co-researchers. I would like to report the following points of view:

"This is a learning place for me. How do you deal with that? I notice when someone shuts someone down, it is so hard to react to this virtually. Face-to-face, I would feel the electricity in the room. I would try to take a break. How do you challenge another person in front of a group/team virtually?"

"I have challenged a person in a situation virtually. It is easier if you have gone through the training [about Virtual Leadership]. It is about creating a culture in the team where it is OK to challenge a person in front of others virtually. It is important to contract about it."

"It is not OK to humiliate a person in public. Hence, you say in the meeting: 'We need to discuss this offline'. This is enough of a signal to everybody. And you do not humiliate the person."

For me, in retrospect, I think that there is a difference between giving challenging (or even confronting – in the positive sense) feedback to a person in a virtual group/team and humiliating the person. Challenging can be positive – even in front of everybody virtually – and does not have to be humiliating. This, in turn, requires skills to confront a person well virtually. I do struggle with the idea that challenging a person can only happen on a one-to-one (offline) basis virtually because this might actually generate a lack of transparency in the group/team. This, in turn, can be disempowering for a group/team, or at least, like in Jeff's case, deprive them of a growth opportunity.

Having said that, I would also like to share Jade's views, another co-researcher, on this specific aspect:

This makes me reflect that people are more sensitive to feedback virtually and do we end up having to give the feedback in front of everybody instead of having the chance to do it individually? Bad behaviour needs to be stopped and it is hard to express it with a tone that is emotionally at the right level when you have to do it in front of others. It is hard to take a break from the meeting virtually and challenge one individual separately as you could easily do in a physical meeting. There you can use a two-layer approach: express what is not right in plenary but then immediately have a one-to-one to debrief and it is usually easier without awkward feelings.

When Thomas was in the grip and then in the flow.
I would like to share a final Critical Incident related to the absence of visuals combined with giving 'power-to' or taking 'power-over'.

Thomas shared the following situation:

We were in a virtual meeting speaking about several strategic initiatives. The meeting attendees were not directly reporting to me, but they needed to deliver on some projects. I was asking about the progress made on some of these initiatives. It was actually a yes/no question: had they achieved something or not? Two people jumped into a long explanation of what they had done. I said: "This was not my question". I soon realised that these two people were trying to rebalance the situation by mentioning all the things that they had done as a way of explaining why they were not ready. I was thinking quietly: (1) "This is not what I asked" (2) "You must think that I am really stupid" (3) "How did they actually interpret the question?" Obviously, they needed to defend themselves, hence my question must have been threatening to them. How could I have turned the question around so that they did not feel that they had to defend themselves? After a short while I decided to turn the situation around and I said: "Great that you have gone through such a long process. My question was: where are we?". They responded by giving me much clearer information about where they were in the process and gave me some clear commitments regarding the actions that they wanted to take. After the meeting I thought: "What was this all about?" If I had exercised my power by confronting them with words, I would have lost it (my power); here it was more about taking them through the motions to get them to commit to clear actions.

TO SUMMARISE

The absence of visuals in the virtual space can be significantly empowering. Leaders and team members will increase their chance of speaking up and stepping into their power if they do not use cameras. The success of their intervention and their 'power-to' though will depend mainly on their capability to identify whether they are 'in the flow' or 'in the grip'.

IMPLICATIONS FOR VIRTUAL LEADERS

In order to identify whether one is 'in the flow' or 'in the grip', leaders need a specific set of skills and competences that are even more critical virtually than face-to-face.

In my view, this last Critical Incident demonstrates clearly the necessary skills and competences in order to own one's own 'power-to' without depriving others of their 'power-to'. We have explored all of these in this chapter, but let's summarise them here:

1. **Self-awareness**: what is actually happening with me right now?

2. **Awareness of the process and psychodynamics**: what is actually happening here in the team? What is going on for them?

3. **Intellectual and emotional empathy**: how did they actually understand the question? And how do they now feel about my intervention?

4. **Versatility:** quickly adapting one's own interventions to maintain own 'power-to'.

5. **Going with the flow**: leading and facilitating virtual meetings requires a particular skill to recognise where the energy is in the discussion so that one can ride the waves of the exchange, galvanise the energy of the contributors in the space while holding the agenda lightly; i.e., not forgetting what the plan and the aims were, but constantly reassessing the best way to go to reach those.

6. **Listening differently**: many people are still very attached to body language and facial expressions and therefore require the use of cameras. My view is that body language has been overestimated and can actually be misleading. The art for virtual leaders and facilitators is more to listen differently by reading the voice of people, which reveals much more than one might think. Multi-layered listening is a technique that everybody can learn (Caulat 2012, pp. 40–41)

7. **Working purposefully against the traditional digital etiquette:**

    a. Bringing the voice of everybody into the space at the beginning of a meeting and considering this moment of establishing the human connection as an integrative part of the meeting.

    b. Asking people to remain unmuted.

    c. Encouraging people to interrupt at any time.

    d. Developing a meeting culture with virtual nodding.

CHAPTER 8 –
Proposition 3: Hierarchical power and technology can cut teams off from their power!

Hierarchical power can be the most limiting factor for organisations in the virtual space and the drama is that collaborative technology seems to be cementing hierarchical power, instead of diluting it.

In this chapter I would like to raise readers' awareness of a phenomenon that I have encountered quite frequently over the last ten years. Many companies have invested time and money in training their middle and senior management in virtual collaboration and virtual leadership. Often, the executive level does not receive any training. As leading and collaborating in the virtual space belongs to a different paradigm compared to face-to-face (Caulat 2012, p. 119), this quickly creates a disconnect between middle and senior management on the one hand and the top executives on the other hand. The former start implementing a different culture of leadership and collaboration while the latter do not know what they don't know and simply transfer on to the virtual space what they do face-to-face. This creates a paralysing gap between the former and the latter, so that middle and senior managers are often confronted with a real dilemma – whether to challenge top management in their views of organisations and collaboration or not. This feels risky and daunting for most of them because the scope of the challenge goes far beyond a single argument and encompasses a whole view of the organisation or even a new view of relationships and work.

Hierarchy exists in any type of organisation!
Before looking at one Critical Incident demonstrating the phenomenon mentioned above, it is important to understand that

hierarchy as a form of organising exists if not explicitly, at least implicitly in any type of organisation. As Galinsky et al. (2008, p. 352) write: "Hierarchy, in its various forms, is prevalent in so many groups and organisations that it appears to be one of the most fundamental features of social relations. [...] Even when hierarchy is minimised by different models of social organising (Fiske, 1992), it is never absent, inevitably emerging both between and within groups (Leavitt, 2005; Sidanius & Pratto, 1999)".

In addition, hierarchy does not only express itself through people at the top of the organisation but also through procedures, processes, structures, systems and rules, to name a few aspects. As Buchanan and Badham write (2010, p. 53) "Power, therefore, is woven into what we take for granted, the order of things, the social and organisation structures in which we find ourselves, the rule systems that appear to constitute the 'natural' running of day-to-day procedures. It is difficult to challenge 'the way things are', or even to recognise in the first place that what one is presented with is an established pattern of power relations and some immutable facet of social life. It is in the interest of those who can manipulate and exploit these taken-for-granted norms that the unequal distribution of power is accepted and not subject to challenge". These lines underline how implicitly embedded power might be in organisations. They also imply that, depending on the culture of the organisation in question, there might be more or less embedded power.

Hierarchical power can paralyse a virtual team.
Bearing the above in mind, let's have a look at the following Critical Incident shared by John:

We had a virtual meeting set up for sixty minutes. We spent the first fifteen minutes waiting for the main decision-maker to join us. He was stuck in another meeting and sent us the following message: "I will be there soon". He finally joined our virtual meeting after twenty minutes; he was excited and emotional and I wondered whether he encountered problems in his previous meeting. He immediately spoke and spoke and we could not stop him. After thirty-five minutes he said that he had to leave earlier because he had a plane to catch. There was no time left for discussion. He said that during that time he was nevertheless able to read what we had prepared. Our sense was that, in the best case, he would have only taken in 30% of the information and that he might forget it soon again. This was a member of our Top Management. The meeting attendees were not at all happy! I was in a real dilemma: should I have stopped this at the very beginning? On the other hand, we needed a quick decision and the time to reschedule might have been too long. We felt that we had prepared for the meeting very well but his behaviour was not acceptable. Afterwards we actually found out that the topic that we wanted to discuss with him was precisely the topic he got challenged upon by the Board.

A very rich discussion followed that Critical Incident at the second inquiry session with the co-researcher group in question. Several questions were raised: would the same have happened face-to-face? Would that person have behaved differently? The dominant view was that it is easier to show bad behaviour virtually than face-to-face because people feel less restrained. Also, I would like to add that during all these years of virtual leadership practice and training, I have learnt that people in the virtual space, much more than face-to-face, tend to project onto others and amplify the emotions that they are going through when they join a new meeting. For example, if before joining our meeting a manager has a difficult conversation and ends up feeling frustrated and angry, their anger and frustration will potentially become even more tangible when they join our meeting and they might even think that we are all frustrated and angry. In our case here, it could simply be that the person in question 'spoke and spoke' precisely because it was in the virtual space with no 'social walls' to restrain him and he needed this to deal with the apparently hard time that he seemed to have had at the previous meeting.

We then explored whether this type of behaviour also depends on the company culture and looked into John's dilemma: *Shall I stop what is happening or not?* Thomas, another member of the inquiry group said that *in his company they cancel meetings if they get delayed by more than five minutes.* Also, the question was raised whether a sufficient 'psychological contract' was made with the top manager in question. He was not trained in virtual collaboration and speaking with him upfront to make him aware of what the requirements for a virtual meeting are, would have been essential.

For example, in the case of John's team, the requirements were that everybody should have read the preparatory document before joining the meeting and that everybody should log into the meeting five minutes before the official start. Having said that, we then reflected on how and whether this type of contracting upfront with top management might be feasible and how much courage it might take to do this, depending on the company culture. We raised the question as to how much a top manager can really get prepared for virtual collaboration, internally from within the company, which would mean explicitly challenging hierarchy because a senior or middle manager would coach a top executive; and how much some external intervention might be needed, particularly in organisations with strong top-down hierarchy.

We carried on exploring and came to the conclusion that the company culture might have a bigger role in the ways hierarchical power plays out in the virtual space than it might do face-to-face. If you want to see these positive changes in virtual collaboration developing, you have to be prepared to challenge these 'bad behaviours' even at the top level. *"Easier said than done!"* some were saying.

We finally concluded by saying that implementing an effective and efficient virtual collaboration etiquette can easily be done (relatively speaking) if all team attendees have been trained. It is also possible to successfully include a newcomer into this new way of working, but it does become more challenging if several new members join the team at once or if a top manager has not been trained and joins the virtual collaboration.

Hierarchical power can take a different form in the virtual space, albeit the impact of it being very similar. Consider the following Critical Incident shared by Lynn:

I was attending a global leadership meeting with the top two hundred leaders. We had breakout sessions with twelve to thirteen people in each. It was a very international group. The topic to discuss in the breakout sessions was straightforward and the first five minutes went really well, with good sharing and exchange of views. One Top Executive joined the breakout group I was in. The exchange stopped. All remained silent and on mute. Cameras were off. Only the Top Executive was not on mute, and everybody was looking up to her for her comments. I was thinking: Should I speak? Should I not? [...]

There is something quite distinct and impactful when a person joins a breakout group after the group has started to form and this gets even more so if the person is more senior in the hierarchy.

The Top Executive joined and greeted everyone. It was not her intention to remain unmuted the whole time. But there was something in the patterns that meant the attendees were expecting her to speak. The whole setting – boss unmuted – others muted – was probably reinforcing these patterns and therefore the hierarchical power.

You could argue that a similar phenomenon might also have taken place in a face-to-face large group event when a figure of authority would join one of the work groups. My experience though is– as Lynn's experience – that this phenomenon clearly gets amplified in the virtual space, precisely because people can mute themselves and switch off cameras. So doing, they send – consciously or unconsciously – the signal that they go into a passive and listening mode; whether this is also a sign of respect or not is almost secondary at this stage. What should be in primary focus is that in so doing, the emerging stifled interaction patterns make any genuine dialogue impossible. Here again, because the top executive did not know what she did not know (i.e., about the amplified impact of joining a virtual break out group), her hierarchical power actually got cemented into the very patterns of the meeting.

For us, the following question remains: how can we invite top managers who do not know what they don't know, to develop a good understanding of the new paradigm of virtual collaboration so that their hierarchical power does not get in the way? What are other options in addition to or as an alternative to training them?

HR has a pivotal role to play in transforming hierarchical power from a liability into an asset in the virtual space.
In order to illustrate further how hierarchy can become a strong limiting – if not paralysing – factor in the virtual space, I would like to share my experience of working with two different companies.

Recently I was working with a global Swedish organisation. The company decided to run a pilot with thirteen of their most senior managers about virtual leadership and virtual collaboration. After the pilot, which was successful, we were asked to work with more groups of senior leaders. All groups were cross-cultural and cross-functional with high levels of diversity. Already after the training with the pilot group and then more so after the following group, we received the feedback from HR that they were somehow irritated because participants in our training had learned about the advantages of not using cameras and some had started implementing this in their team and with colleagues. This was going against what the Board of the company had been preaching, namely that the use of cameras was a 'must' as a sign of respect for good relationships. Actually, some participants had mentioned this company rule to me during the preparatory interviews and we explored where this rule was coming from. Two main arguments became apparent. The first was the transfer of a habit from the face-to-face into the virtual space; people were feeling more comfortable and on more familiar ground if they could see their counterparts on camera. The second was that managers felt that they had better control over what people were doing during the meeting and liked to believe that by using cameras they could avoid multitasking in meetings. At this stage, I would like to refer to my argument on page 33 (i.e., my question to my reader here is: please, be honest with yourself, how many times have you been watching a person in a meeting or in a public speech, looking focused on what they say, but actually with your mind wandering miles away with thousands of questions, such as "When will this monologue end? Will I manage to get my shopping done tonight? etc."). We like to believe that we can control people if we see them, but actually we can't, and the virtual space makes this very clear to us.

I had to work intensively with HR who, in the spirit of not wanting to rock the boat too much, first attempted to convince me to work with cameras in the training. I decided not to collude with this wish because I was convinced that I would not serve the organisation well by doing that. After a series of meetings with HR, in which I tried to explain the research that I had been doing and what I had learnt from my own practice, the global HR team leader decided to organise a training with us because the global HR team had become interested and keen to understand for themselves what was going on. The training with this team of highly experienced HR professionals went well and a vast majority opened up to practices of virtual collaboration that were indeed challenging what they had done so far virtually, and they decided to experiment with these. However, it was their collective decision not to challenge top management explicitly on the use of cameras, but actually to keep maintaining flexibility as to when to use cameras or not. While I fully understand and support the wish not to be dogmatic about using or not using cameras, my challenge to HR was – and would still be now – to explicitly confront top management with their beliefs and practices in order to fully support the implementation of a new virtual collaboration culture in the company.

The same phenomenon happened with a global German company that I was working with a few years ago. We had the opportunity to train several executive leaders of the organisation, but not all. Since the organisation was a very wide one, the training at the top level did not have sufficient reach to have a systemic impact on top management as a whole. However, the training did have a systemic impact on the senior and middle management levels (approx. seventy people were trained) and after a few months, many of the senior and middle managers trained were rather frustrated; they were implementing what they had learnt in the training – which was going far beyond the use of cameras and included different communication styles, different meeting procedures, a different use of technology, etc. – and starting to develop very successfully a new collaboration culture. However, they were slowed down and at times almost stopped by top management who did not know what they did not know and either ignored the new practice or even ridiculed it as strange and illogical. In this case, HR which was part of the training (several HR responsible all over the world had joined one group of managers as individuals and actively participated in the learning), decided to take measures to mitigate this frustration and disconnect between top management and senior and middle management. They developed so-called 'guidelines' for virtual collaboration that were posted on the intranet and actively communicated within the organisation. So doing, they were giving permission to the managers and leaders trained to challenge their untrained counterparts by referring to these guidelines and inviting them to implement the new virtual collaboration practice. In the worst case, these guidelines were giving them (at least) permission to start a conversation about virtual collaboration and, in so doing, challenge the status quo and **speak up.** This example shows how a relatively simple measure can break up paralysing hierarchical power. The guidelines tackle new ways of doing things and new procedures based on a different world view and enable leaders to recover their 'power-to' by challenging the power that top management implicitly had over them and inviting the latter to enter a new paradigm of collaboration.

At this stage, you might argue that actually any type of change and/or training intervention might be very difficult if top management is not involved from the start; you are probably right. What makes this issue much more critical though is that managers going through such training will inevitably challenge existing views from the face-to-face paradigm by implementing practices more in line with the virtual paradigm and, in so doing, challenge an organisation at its very core. The problem is that top management often consider virtual collaboration and virtual leadership to be only technical knowledge with 'tips and tricks' that you can learn. They completely underestimate the true dimension of the change required to make virtual collaboration and virtual leadership really work and therefore realise only later – if at all – that they need to be involved in the changes in question. In other words, they invest the money and time of their leaders so that the latter learn a different virtual collaboration and leadership and themselves become the stumbling block of their own efforts because they don't know what they don't know.

Communication technologies often cement hierarchical power.
While technology has made huge progress in the last ten years and radically changed the landscape of collaboration, it has in fact changed the way people actually work together only to a certain extent. Recently, one of my clients in the telecommunication sector argued that, in spite of huge technological progress, for some reason managers seem to be limited in their capabilities to envision a different type of collaboration virtually; this might be correct to some degree. I would argue differently and claim that many virtual collaboration platforms are paradoxically getting in the way of leaders fully exploiting the potential of the virtual space, precisely because they cement traditional hierarchy in their inherent

structure and design. Let's have a look at the following screenshot from one of the leading technology suppliers in virtual collaboration.

WebEx

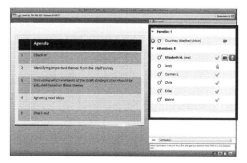 

As you can see above, the simple set-up of the plenary resembles traditional hierarchy patterns. On the right-hand side, you have the so-called 'panellists' and 'presenters', namely the ones who present and 'tell' and underneath you have the 'attendees', who are the ones who listen and ask questions. Is this set-up with such categories necessary? Furthermore, the same platform calls the features that they entail 'privileges', itself a word with a strong hierarchical connotation. Hence, for example, the panellist who presents and/or leads the discussion (often the team leader or a person higher up in the hierarchy) has the power to enable (in a technical sense) the attendees to raise their hands if they wish to speak (by clicking on the corresponding symbol on the platform). They also have the power to mute a person (for example if the background is too loud) or to mute the whole group or team if they want to present undisturbed. On the other hand, they can give permission to attendees to move from one slide to the other at their own speed and independently of the rest of the group. However, particularly regarding the latter feature, most 'presenters' decide not to activate it, which means that 'attendees' can only view the slide that the 'presenter' is commenting on at a given moment. The latter is even informed by a specific sign (!) when an attendee is not watching the slide that the 'presenter' is commenting on and might be viewing something else on their computer. These examples show how technology in this case is intrinsically driven by traditional forms of hierarchy, promoting a culture of 'telling' rather than one of dialogue, and actually giving leaders a false sense of control. I claim that this is a false sense of control for the following reason: it is not because a person views the slide that the 'presenter' is talking about at a given moment that they are actually listening. Paradoxically, by giving a false sense of control and 'power-over' attendees, these types of features actually lead to increased multitasking among attendees, who might more quickly lose their interest in what is being discussed and start writing emails or doing something else. In this case, you could ask: who has power over whom? While the attendees might not be really enabled to speak up and step into their 'power-to', the panellists might become victims of the illusion of control and lose their 'power-over' as well as their 'power-to' as a result, without even noticing it.

Further virtual collaboration platforms (see Appendix 4) are designed in a very similar way. As you can see on the next page, platforms such as MS Teams or Adobe Connect have a similar plenary layout with the hierarchy of 'presenters', 'hosts' and 'participants' or 'presenters' and 'attendees'. MS Teams calls their different features that might be activated or deactivated by the presenter 'permissions' and Adobe Connect uses the same terminology as WebEx: 'privileges'. Zoom might have in comparison with the three former platforms a less obvious hierarchical structure (see fourth screen shot on page 66); however, they also have features called 'securities' that can be deactivated so that only the host can share their screen, or the host can decide to mute everybody, for example.

MS Teams

Adobe Connect

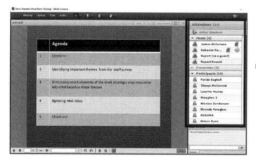

Zoom

Before moving on with my reflection, I would like to emphasise that my aim with the above discourse is not to demonise any virtual collaboration platform. It is much more to urge leaders not to be seduced by the false power that they might see in these platforms, but to start reflecting on the impact of these features far beyond the functional and to realise the power dynamics that they might create.

Powerful or powerless in the 'chat'?

A very interesting feature on most virtual collaboration platforms is the 'chat' area. People can connect with any other attendee (or group of attendees) in the meeting/event and send them written messages. They can do that without the meeting leader or facilitator having access to it. Most of the time, more informal conversations evolve in the chat, while the more formal conversation takes place verbally as spoken words. Having observed the chat phenomenon, I would claim that the chat conversation is similar to the conversation that meeting attendees would have during the coffee break, with the only (and very important) difference being that the chat conversation happens simultaneously, in other words in parallel to the spoken conversation. Or, we could say that formal and informal conversations happen at the same time, as opposed to a meeting in the face-to-face environment where the informal conversations happen consecutively, i.e., in the break and not during the meeting. While the informal conversations during the coffee break might have some influence or not – at least to some extent – on the subsequent parts of the meeting face-to-face, the interesting aspect is that the simultaneous informal conversations in the chat area seldom enter the formal spoken conversation. Often, I observe that as a matter of fact, they are two parallel conversations. This is where power dynamics might be at play. Which conversation is the most important one: the 'formal' (spoken) one led by the team leader or facilitator or the more informal one, unfolding in the chat? Also, I wonder: why do people have the need to chat with each other in parallel to the meeting? Is it that they do not dare to say out loud what they think? What is it in the way that the virtual meeting gets facilitated that leads people to prefer to use the chat? In my experience, the chat is more spontaneous and 'informal' and it seems that people use the chat room when the spoken conversation in the virtual meeting becomes too stifled or too sterile.

Here again, when leaders do not know what they don't know about the virtual space as a new paradigm, they let themselves become cemented in their hierarchical power of the discourse mainly shaped as 'telling' while the 'chatters' often get stuck in 'gossiping'. All of this is not very conducive to genuine dialogue. Having said that, if leaders are aware of the fact that virtual collaboration belongs to another paradigm of communication, they can learn how to shape different power dynamics and weave the two unfolding conversations into a real dialogue. This requires a collective agreement in the team or in the group in question about how the chat area should and should not be used or/and a conscious plan of the dialogue where the use of the chat area will be designed as an inherent part of the spoken conversation.

The one who invites has the power!
As a consequence of what we explored above, I would like to underline that the one who invites others to his/her technological platform and sets up the meeting has the 'power-to'. When leaders want to influence peers, stakeholders or even external parties such as customers or suppliers, they will need to consciously set up the meeting. In addition to specifying the attendee list, setting up the

agenda and sending the calendar invitations, they will need to consciously plan the process that they want to take for the discussion. They will also need to choose the appropriate features of the platform and decide how to use those. So doing, they will foster the right atmosphere and culture for the exchange.

Let me conclude this reflection about technology in virtual collaboration with the words of Jarvenpaa and Keating (2021, p. 2): "Digital technology masks these differences or leaves them easily misunderstood. [...] We argue that these moments of breakdown are a result of how our technological understanding is moving faster than communication understanding. [...] Global teams need a better understanding of how communication works to capitalise on what technological innovations in communication allow". I would actually go further in the argument and claim that any leader of virtual or hybrid teams (these do not necessarily need to be global teams) do need to develop a much better understanding of how communication works in the virtual space if they want to retain their 'power-to' and enable their team members to step into their 'power-to'.

TO SUMMARISE

It is essential that leaders conscientiously reflect about the features that technology offers them to shape their communication and leadership and deliberately make their choice of the appropriate features, which will promote a collaboration culture of 'speaking up' and enable others to step into their 'power-to'.

Top managers or executives who have not been trained to lead virtually and simply transfer on to the virtual space what they do face-to-face might represent the biggest threat to virtual collaboration because, without realising it, their hierarchical power embedded in technology, procedures and ways of working might stifle any exchange and cut everybody off from their 'power-to' speak up.

IMPLICATIONS FOR VIRTUAL LEADERS

Leaders need to realise that virtual collaboration and virtual leadership belong to a different paradigm. If they want to help their organisation develop, they need to move from a place where they do not know what they don't know – to one where they know what they don't know and want to learn about it. This will require humility, curiosity, and experimentation. HR managers and OD practitioners have an essential role to play in this transition and cannot simply let things emerge.

CHAPTER 9 –
Proposition 4: Knowledge and expertise as important sources of power in the virtual space

Knowledge and expertise are clear, fundamental and specific sources of power in the virtual space; they are actually much more distinctive sources of power in the virtual space than face-to-face.

Expertise and/or knowledge have been repeatedly mentioned as among the main sources of power in the literature about power in the traditional leadership paradigm. Whether you look into the French and Raven model (1958, pp. 259–69) or whether you look into the Benfari et al. model (1986, pp. 12–16), expertise and knowledge/information are mentioned as one of six sources of power (according to French and Raven) or one of the eight sources of power according to Benfari et al.

For me it was very interesting that knowledge and expertise emerged so clearly during the Action Inquiry research as a significant and main source of power in the virtual space. My co-researchers clearly believed that having the expertise and/or knowledge on any given subject matter would help them gain 'power-to' and 'power-over' others, as a result.

Steve loses his 'power-to' because he is not the expert.
Let's start with a Critical Incident showing how the lack of expertise might strongly get in the way of people trying to speak up and be heard. Steve shared the following:

I was attending one of our Executive Team meetings. I tried to contribute to business issues. Nobody acknowledged my points. There was a silence after I had spoken and then the conversation was moved on as if I had not been heard. I started to doubt myself. Nobody was building on my points and, as a result, I withdrew. Silence in the virtual space kills me. Face-to-face you see the body language, and this feels less disabling to me. Also, if it would have been an HR topic, then I would have been fearless. I would have said something like: "Guys, we have got to go back here. I was not heard!". If I have the expertise, then I am fearless. If not, then I quickly get unsure. After the meeting I did not get any reaction from my colleagues either.

In spite of his wide experience Matthew cannot gain 'power-to' because he does not frame it well.
In the same vein, one might have knowledge and expertise but not be able to offer it in such a way that it can be embraced – meaning the person in question might not be able to step into their 'power-to'. This is very well described with the Critical Incident shared by Matthew:

Last year we (four of us based in Barcelona, Seattle and Switzerland) were working on a project to define research questions to submit to a group of researchers in charge of carrying out a survey. It took us time to get in-tune with one another. We wanted different things. We had three or four rounds. It was a kind of peer-to-peer work because we all had the same level of budget. We had to get the terms of reference sorted and to get the research questions right. I was of the opinion that we ought to keep the questions in broad terms first and that we would fine tune afterwards. The person in Seattle thought this was sloppy. I thought: "I have done it before!". There was an exchange of emails. I thought that I would let it go and allow the person to get her thing. I felt at the same time: (1) I will let it go, (2) frustrated that I was not able to articulate my experience in a way that others could embrace it. [...] We ran the first round of the survey, and we got a lot of feedback from the researchers that they could not answer the questions and things got classified differently. We now need to go through another round, and we absolutely need to get the questions right this time. [...] When you work in such a context with no clear hierarchy, you have to be more subtle with how you influence others. It is about framing my own experience in a way that does not come across as too bold. You cannot rely completely on the logical level.

Paul did not speak up because he did not have the facts.

The following Critical Incident shared by Paul is, in my view, very representative of frequent cases that I have observed. It shows precisely how the lack of knowledge might feel disempowering in the virtual space and prevent people from speaking up:

> *I was attending a virtual meeting with the commercial council. X., the leader of the meeting, started speaking to one of the Directors, saying to him: "You are the market leader. You should know it better!" Then came several words, negative words, that I can't remember. Then a big silence followed. It felt very heavy. I still remember this heaviness very well. Then, the meeting moved on and other topics were discussed. In that moment, I asked myself: "Should I have intervened?" I kept quiet. I had no facts. It was so harsh! I felt that X. left no space for anything else to be said. I decided to keep quiet.*

In the above case, which certainly reveals a lot of team dynamics at play, my co-researchers and I explored whether the situation would have unfolded in a different way, i.e., whether Paul would have intervened, had the meeting taken place face-to-face. The main view was that face-to-face, Paul might have tried to read other people's minds by looking at their faces and that he might have found some encouragement in speaking up, even without having any facts. As he mentioned, *the silence felt very heavy;* my experience is that silence gets amplified in the virtual space and indeed feels heavier as a result. Hence the hurdle that Paul had to overcome might have felt too high and risky, particularly because clear hierarchical power was playing a role.

Norman uses his knowledge to get a decision revisited in a virtual context with heavy hierarchical power.

Now let's have a look at Norman's Critical Incident showing how knowledge can eventually help one to speak up and gain 'power-over' those higher in the hierarchy.

> *Our business in my region brought excellent results last year. We were seen as 'heroes' of profitability! We have now received new targets for 2021. These targets were set top-down by the Group, and they are nearly impossible to achieve. The President and the CFO informed me and the further two General Managers in my region:*

they showed the targets and the way they were split. Compared to the usual target meetings face-to-face, when we would have two hours and our points of view would have been listened to and built upon, this time, we were only given thirty minutes. Then President and the CFO asked: "OK guys, what do you think?". It felt as if their only purpose was simply to tell us. We as General Managers agreed that the targets were not making any sense. We simply felt that the targets and their split were impossible to reach. It got very emotional: you could see and feel all the emotions going on. Then suddenly the President said: "Guys, the target given by the Group is what it is." You could observe the struggle of emotions and power at the same time. Actually, each of us had a point. Even the point "the targets are what they are" was a legitimate point. We asked the President to go back to the Group and push back on these unrealistic challenges. This was a clear no go.

In our Inquiry Group, we reflected on what made the meeting so specific and so specifically different. First, we identified the duration of the meeting, which was much shorter than a meeting in the face-to-face environment. Did the President and CFO keep the meeting short on purpose? Would they have done the same face-to-face? Probably not! Norman thought that he and the other General Managers were not given enough time. Norman also reflected on the fact that his own words (as well as those of the other General Managers) were stronger, less measured: *"Face-to-face, we would have been more in control of our emotions and more cautious with our words."*

Norman's Critical Incident developed further:

The power went back to us because we, as General Managers, explained to the President and the CFO that our local teams would not agree to the goals, taking into consideration that the goals were closely linked to their yearly bonus and that they would never agree to goals that were impossible to reach as this would mean that they would not get any bonus. My push back was: "Well, if the goals are what they are, then you need to help us to communicate these to the local teams. You should also consider lowering the threshold for the bonus." I was sharing my local knowledge of the market and giving them details that the President and the CFO simply could not ignore.

It was as if showing our expertise (as General Managers) and our knowledge of the local market shifted the power dynamics. In the end, the President and the CFO agreed to go back to the Group and negotiate the threshold for the bonus.

Norman told the Inquiry Group that, *after ten days, he and the other General Managers received an email confirming that top management had decided to lower the threshold even more than he was asking for and the other targets were also lowered beyond what he would have hoped for.* In my view, this Critical Incident shows very clearly how, in spite of embedded hierarchical power in well-engineered settings, Norman and his peers were able – through their knowledge of the local market – to shift the power dynamics and to step into their 'power-to' push back and get decisions that were a fait accompli revisited and amended.

The reflection work we did in Norman's inquiry group after exploring the Critical Incident that he shared brought up a very important point. Knowledge and expertise are a more necessary source of power in the virtual space than in the face-to-face, however they are not sufficient. Norman observed: *"I can witness lots of digital meetings in the new normal these days; and some of them are presented by experts in the field; yet a total 'disaster' in the outcome."* We explored that this source of power needs to be combined with virtual leadership skills to really give 'power-to'; this is what the Critical Incident shared by Matthew (see page 72) shows. Julia added: *"I think having subject expertise might make it easier [...], maybe you can 'get away' with some things if people already respect your leadership given your knowledge?".*

As mentioned above, I was at first somewhat surprised to hear how knowledge and expertise were seen by my co-researchers as such a clear and specific source of power in the virtual space – actually a much more distinctive one than in the face-to-face environment. My reading of wider research on the topic after the work I did with my co-researchers showed that knowledge emerges as a clear source of power in the virtual space. Panteli and Tucker, who researched power dynamics in eighteen globally distributed teams (2009, p. 2), shared the following results: "Several interviewees described the power within their team as originating from knowledge and noted that at any given point in time the most powerful was the individual with the most relevant information". It is essential to note at this stage that Panteli and Tucker (2009, p. 3) found out that power therefore was a shifting phenomenon, as it would move flexibly on to the person who had the necessary and relevant knowledge at a given point of time: "[...] knowledge is becoming the source of power in the current digital age and this power moves to the knowledge source". Norman's case above clearly demonstrates this!

TO SUMMARISE

Compared to face-to-face, knowledge and expertise seem to be even more critical and fundamental in the virtual space, for team members, managers and leaders to step into their 'power-to' and speak up. However, knowledge and expertise are necessary but not sufficient! This source of power needs to be combined with versatile skills of communication as well as process awareness.

IMPLICATIONS FOR VIRTUAL LEADERS

More than face-to-face, leaders need to be well prepared for their virtual interventions. Showing that they have the knowledge and/or expertise will be an essential asset for their 'power-to'. However, they will need to learn how to engage their colleagues, superiors and team members with their knowledge and expertise. They will need to move away from the traditional presentation that they might have given in a face-to-face environment – towards highly interactive meetings where input or information is shared and read asynchronously (see Glossary) and discussions, as well as decisions, will take place synchronously (see Glossary), based on strong dialogic processes to ensure a high level of engagement among attendees. In other words, leaders will need to reconfigure the way they share their knowledge and expertise in the virtual space if they want to capitalise on this essential source of power.

CHAPTER 10 –
Proposition 5: Language is ACTION with power, not power in action!

In the virtual space, non-native speakers might lose some of their 'power-to', but native speakers might lose it just as much if they do not use language differently.

Leaders can develop a dialogic culture of engagement in the virtual space, one that will enable team members to overcome potential power differentials related to language and step into their 'power-to'. For this, they will need to become 'facileaders'.

In this chapter, I would like to show how a good command of the chosen language of collaboration (English for most cases) remains a main source of power in the virtual space – even if it seems obvious – and how we need to use language differently virtually in order to transform this source of power into a positive and productive one.

Marschan et al. (1997, pp. 591–593) claimed that language as a taken-for-granted element has almost disappeared from research, even though it emerges as one of the crucial aspects in multicultural teams. I would have tended to agree with that, even though some of my co-researchers actually decided to focus on this specific aspect in the context of our research. For them the key question was: does the fact that the official language of the team you belong to is your native language or not, impact on your 'power-to' in virtual collaboration?

Many readers will now think: "Of course it does! What a stupid question!". Our findings and my experience actually show that the answer to this question is more subtle, certainly not black and white and entails interesting potential.

Sarah's team members were not bothered to ask questions, even if they did not understand.

Let's start with one Critical Incident shared by Sarah:

> We had a team meeting (across regions). I was paying attention to the people in my team, whether they were asking questions or not. All the people in my team except one had English as second language. After the meeting, I reflected with my team members and some of them admitted that sometimes they did not understand what was being said, but that they would make their decision as to whether they should ask a clarification question or not dependent on who was actually speaking at the time: is it the big boss or a colleague? Even among the colleagues, they would reflect whether they would feel comfortable asking a question or not. In addition, many of them admitted: "After a full day (they were working across time zones), I am just tired and I can't be bothered to ask clarification questions".

This echoes something that another co-researcher Patrick (Chinese, non-native speaker of English) also shared:

> In virtual meetings, particularly when we have a mix of connections, with people sitting around the same table and others like me linked in virtually, I often don't dare to ask a clarifying question because I do not know how this will be interpreted by the rest of the team. Face-to-face, I would approach the person that I did not completely understand during the coffee break and ask them to elaborate more about what they said. Virtually, I would be hesitant about holding up the rest of the team.

Here one could actually argue: who has power over whom? Which power do I actually have if people do not understand me, but actually do not want to let me know?

Méndez García and Pérez Cañado (2005) intend to raise new awareness on the essential role of language in multicultural teams, so do Nurmi et al (2009, p. 6), who carried out thorough qualitative research with four virtual teams: "Language skills had a significant effect on communication ability increasing the power dynamics in the teams. People with limited English skills had less influencing power in the teams than native speakers. Their ability to argue and state reasons for their opinions were limited. [...] Non-native English speakers considered themselves powerless when fighting for one's own ideas in English with a native speaker."

Obviously, as Nurmi et al. describe above, not mastering the team's official language can negatively impact on your 'power-to'. Sarah from our research group also shared her observations of international virtual meetings with groups of fifteen managers who were peers, i.e., all at the same hierarchical level, where native speakers would inevitably speak first and non-native speakers would speak up later on in the meeting. This absolutely corresponds with my own experience of running virtual workshops or virtual summits with international teams: I always need to plan my facilitation in a way that cuts across this phenomenon, so that non-native speakers do speak sooner. This is particularly important in groups which are not aware of this phenomenon and where native speakers would simply speak because nobody else is speaking and wonder afterwards why it is like that.

Native speakers can also be hindered by their own native language in the virtual space!
In the same way that non-native speakers can struggle to get into their 'power-to', native speakers might also be hindered in virtual collaboration, precisely by their own native language (assuming that this is English in teams where English is the official language). Many leaders with English as their 'mother tongue' who are experienced in leading virtually will explain that they have needed to learn to speak what they call 'international English'. This means an English with no idioms and deprived of any colloquial or too sophisticated expressions, so that they could actually be understood by non-native speakers and have a productive conversation with them. In such situations, the combination of hierarchical power (in a boss-subordinate relationship) and the fact that the boss is a native speaker, and the subordinate is not, works exponentially in cutting subordinates off in their 'power-to' if the boss is not consciously working against it. Having said that, I would claim that the situation is actually more complicated than that and goes far beyond 'speaking international English'.

I have learnt through my many years of training and coaching virtual leaders that, particularly the ones who feel that they need to be subtle with their language and give feedback in a more indirect way, in an effort not to hurt the recipient of the message, actually often lose their 'power-to' in virtual teams that include non-native speakers.

Therefore, leaders need to find a way to speak in a direct, yet respectful and sensitive fashion. In this regard, let's have a look at what Jarvenpaa and Keating (2021, p. 7) found out in their research of global virtual teams: "[...] native English speakers [feel that they] need to attend to the common practice of speaking indirectly because doing so is more 'polite'; the unintended sensitivity leads to ambiguity in their communication and therefore to misunderstandings of instructions, directives, and needs. This form of politeness, which is used to ensure that a request does not threaten the autonomy or the 'face' (i.e., the respect, honour, and social standing) of other team members, can be shown in other ways. [...] a non-native English speaker benefits from a simpler, more direct syntax and approach."

Furthermore, Jarvenpaa and Keating clearly show that in order for leaders to exercise their 'power-to' in an effective way virtually, they ought to shift their understanding of communication as 'knowledge transfer' (when a person does not act on what you intended them to do, you simply give them more information in different ways, under the assumption that if they did not act in the first place, it is because they were lacking information) to an understanding of communication as ACTION. Communication as ACTION means two essential things:

A- I need to make a clear effort to understand how my team member thinks and communicates, "Taking the perspective of others requires explicit recognition of and attentiveness to the hearer. It requires giving up the information transfer model and other models that focus only on the speaker [...] Marketers and advertisers are well aware of this need and spend significant sums of money to find out about their 'hearers'. Everyday virtual team interactions that are task oriented should be no different." Jarvenpaa and Keating (2001, p. 7)

B- I need to phrase my intentions in a clear way. For example, if I said to my team member: "I do not like this feature", the latter might understand it as a preference and not necessarily as a directive. If I say instead: "Please substitute this feature with a different one", my team member will more likely understand these words as a clear directive and actually act on it. Another very common mistake that I observe again and again in the virtual space is the use of WE instead of YOU. Many leaders believe that their directive will be received better if they package it in the following way: "We need to make sure that we inform the customer about this potential delay", whereas what they actually mean is: "Peter, please inform the customer about this potential delay." The use of WE in such a context leads to confusion and certainly does not generate any proactivity in the virtual team.

Hence, by basing my communication on a more accurate understanding of how my team member actually understands what I say and how s/he communicates and by being more direct and precise, yet respectful in the way I frame my messages, I **actually take action** in the sense that (a) I make the active effort to project myself into my team member's shoes and (b) I generate an action on the part of my team member. So doing, I exercise my 'power-to' in an effective manner in the virtual space. In this perspective, language clearly becomes ACTION, which in turn increases my 'power-to'. It also shows that the general understanding and assumptions about the power of language need to be radically revisited.

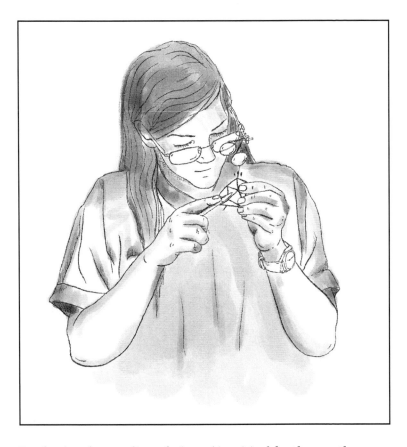

Leaders' understanding of a 'team' is critical for the way they use language and has a strong impact on their 'power-to' in the virtual space.

Leaders might also significantly raise their 'power-to' if they first become aware of their understanding of the 'team' as organisational form. In their very powerful research based on forty-five in-depth interviews and nine global teams, Gibbs et al (2021, p. 10) clearly show the differences in team understanding and what they call 'orientation to participation' and the significant impact this might have on team dynamics and power in the team. Gibbs et al. look into three main team orientations: Help, Learn and Engage

> **Help:** Members who expressed this orientation tended to regard the teams as knowledge repositories and their job as the dissemination

of knowledge, often assumed a more empowered, higher status position, and they viewed the teams as repositories to which they made deposits of knowledge. "Our findings also highlight the subtlety of ethnocentrism and how even the best-intentioned managers and organisational members (such as those with the Help orientation) may inadvertently disparage or discount the views of others and perpetuate status differences." (Gibbs et al, 2021, p. 17)

Learn: The Learn orientation is characterised by a similar, but opposite, one-way flow of knowledge. In this orientation, the team was regarded as a way to learn from the expertise of others, with the global team seen as knowledge repository or database.

Engage: "Although the Help and Learn orientations seemed opposite, both shared the perception of knowledge sharing as a one-way informational flow in which participants saw their role as either provider (Help) or recipient (Learn). In contrast, the Engage orientation was mutually constitutive, bidirectional, and collaborative. Although demanding the most investment by members, it also seemed to deliver the greatest payoffs ..." [...] the Engage orientation coincided with a sense of meaning and importance. Team members expressing this orientation were characterised by a sense of excitement about participating and by a collaborative approach to sharing knowledge. In their approach, responses collectively built upon each other, with the entire team contributing to each given interaction, rather than just being either a 'provider' or a 'recipient'." (Gibbs et al, 2021, p. 17)

Gibbs et al. (2021, p. 15) come to the following conclusion: "[...] our findings do not support reifying status; rather, status differences are dynamic and intersectional features of global team interaction that are malleable and shaped by team communication practices [...] our findings suggest that status differences are socially constructed and thus malleable and can be overcome with team communication practices promoting engagement."

The form of engagement that they promote is precisely based on the assumption that everybody in the team – independently of their status and level of language fluency – has something to contribute and can develop strong synergies resulting in strong motivation and high performance in the virtual team. This form of engagement is **dialogue,** which if well facilitated does help to overcome status differences. At this point, I would like to remind readers of the importance of understanding the technology and how to use the available features in a way that actually enable a dialogic practice and do not reinforce status differences and participation orientations such as 'Help' or 'Learn' (see pages 62–68).

TO SUMMARISE

While the power of language (mastering the official language of the team) certainly needs to remain at the forefront of awareness when leaders navigate through virtual communication, being a non-native speaker with limited language mastery does not have to be an impediment. Leaders can develop a **dialogic culture** of engagement that will enable team members to overcome potential power differentials related to language and step into their 'power-to'. So doing, leaders themselves will strengthen their power and step into their 'power-with' in virtual leadership.

IMPLICATIONS FOR VIRTUAL LEADERS

- In order to enable team members to step into their 'power-to', leaders will need to strengthen their awareness of language as a source of power in the virtual space.

- Leaders will actively work against power differentials in their virtual teams if they shift from an understanding of communication as transfer of information to an understanding of communication as ACTION. This means learning to communicate in a straight, yet respectful way, from the perspective of the recipient. This requires active efforts and specific skills.

- Leaders need to reflect in depth on their understanding of what a 'team' actually is. They need to shift from a place of helping by sharing information or from a place of learning by encouraging all to learn from each other to a place of ENGAGING based on the assumption that everybody in the team (including themselves) has something to bring to the virtual table. They need to develop patterns of building on each other through an active process of listening, in order to actually understand (instead of listening to ask the next clever question) to generate a genuine dialogue. This in turn will require that leaders take a step back and first reflect on the features of the virtual collaboration platform that they use and make a conscious choice on the ones not to use, the ones to use, and how to use them to promote dialogic communication.

- A further implication of all the above is that leaders will also need to strengthen their capabilities to facilitate and lead at the same time. This means that they need to become a '*facileader*' (Caulat, 2012, pp. 80–81), in the sense that they will need to enable team members to develop dialogic skills. The virtual space requires from the leader that s/he makes it easy for their team members to engage with each other and to find new ways of relating with one another, given that the virtual space presents new parameters. This would correspond to the notion of 'facilitation' in its original sense, namely from the Latin 'facilis' (easy) or the French 'faciliter' (to render easy)*. It is as if the leader has to *facil*-itate to enable others to connect effectively in the virtual space and overcome power dynamics, while at the same time **leading** the conversation and giving direction: the virtual leader as a '**facileader**'. In so doing, virtual leaders will increase their power and move swiftly from 'power-to' to 'power-with'.

---

* To facilitate: 1610s, from French faciliter "to render easy" from Latin facilis "easy" (see facile). http://www.etymoline.com Online Etymology Dictionary

CHAPTER 11 –
Proposition 6: When silence speaks up

Silence can be an essential source of power and, if leaders learn how to use it well, they can significantly increase their 'power-to' and, as a result, their 'power-with'.

Most of the time, silence is pregnant with data, and tapping skillfully into silence might reveal invaluable information. However, what I notice in virtual meetings, is that managers tend to get nervous if there is a moment of silence. Often silence is seen as something 'wrong' or unpleasant to say the least – something that needs to be 'fixed'. These unpleasant moments often get swiftly ironed out by sentences such as: "Well, silence means agreement, hence I will move on" or "Has anyone got a question?" – a closed question in itself that does not fulfil its purpose and, on the contrary, shuts people up.

We ought to consider the following aspects (Caulat, 2012 p. 30):
- Silence is actually an integrative part of a conversation and there is nothing wrong with it.

- Everything gets amplified in the virtual space, hence one minute of silence face-to-face will feel like four minutes of silence virtually.

- Silence is a very important part of discourse. For example, people with an Introvert Preference (by 'Introvert' I mean a person who needs some quiet space to think on their own before making up their mind, as opposed to a person with an 'Extravert Preference', who would seek an exchange with others in order to become clearer about what they think – see Glossary) do need silence in order to specify their thinking. Also, silence is seen as a sign of respect in some cultures. For instance, 'silence' usually expresses harmony and respect among Japanese people, but silence is not accorded the same meaning in western cultures (Panteli and Fineman, 2006, pp. 347–352)

- Silence seldom means agreement! It might even imply the opposite.

Remaining silent might be a good strategy to protect one's power.
First of all, let's look into two Critical Incidents from my co-researchers showing how deciding to remain silent actually gave the power back to the protagonists, or even helped them to protect it from the outset.

Paul, member of an executive team, shared the following incident:

Last week, we had a meeting with the mother company. It was an executive meeting and I was proud to present the results from our part of the company. AB (the new CEO) said: "Fantastic, but it does not matter anymore because the truth of the matter is that the market did not grow and you will have to lay people off". He did not listen. He did not ask any questions. Instead, he calculated the number of people that I would have to lay off. I was feeling like a child. If I would have spoken, I would have said something stupid. Hence, I decided to shut up. Everybody else was silent. The new Operations manager eventually made a comment to fill the silence. In that instance, arguing would have made me lose power. AB himself was a victim; he felt the pressure from the company. I thought after a while: "He is scared". He did not understand what was going on with me because he was simply too busy with himself.

I would particularly like to focus on the sentence "*I was feeling like a child. If I would have spoken, I would have said something stupid. Hence, I decided to shut up.*" There is something humiliating in the situation described above and the way it unfolded; I can imagine that, particularly in the virtual setting, this humiliation must have felt very difficult to cope with. Paul actually demonstrated a lot of self-awareness as well as process awareness in this case and decided not to speak up as a way to protect himself from losing his power. In this specific situation, we can even ask the question: who had power over whom? Paul reflected on AB, the CEO, and said: *"He was simply too busy with himself and he was led by his own uncertainties and fears probably without really being aware of those".* Was he in the grip (see pages 42–49)? Possibly. What we can claim for sure is that AB did not have a full grasp of what was going on for Paul and – I would even go so far as to say – of what was going on for the further team members. He was not in his 'power-to' convey a constructive message and had certainly no 'power-over' Paul. Was Paul in his 'power-to'? We do not know because we do not know what his colleagues thought about him in that specific moment: did Paul manage to protect his power in their eyes, or did he come across as 'weak' because he remained silent? We can safely assume that AB did not think much about Paul in that moment because "he was simply too busy with himself." It would have been highly interesting to hear from AB what he thought in retrospect regarding the meeting. Paradoxically, it seems though that by not trying to defend his power in that specific situation, Paul managed to protect it, at least during the meeting.

The second Critical Incident also shows how choosing to remain silent actually increased Thomas's power.

> *I was in a virtual meeting with my successor from my previous team as well as with other colleagues. My successor said: "This was not in order. And I have put that in order". In that moment, it felt like he was criticising my work as his predecessor in the team, and also as if he wanted to shine by saying what he had already sorted out. I consciously decided not to come in and defend myself. I let others judge for themselves. I was thinking: "Will it have an impact if I say nothing, or will this be interpreted as a weakness?" I knew that some colleagues would think: "The fact that Thomas doesn't comment shows that this person (the successor) is quite junior. Thomas is positioning himself as not touchable". I decided that there was no value in defending what I did. In that moment, I felt that by not speaking I was actually establishing my own power.*

Here again, the incident showed how self-awareness and process awareness (see Glossary) were both playing a strong role in Thomas's decision not to step in. Thomas concludes by saying: "I was actually establishing my own power". Obviously, as we look at power as something relational and not a thing (see page 11), we can argue that, because we do not know what the further attendees of the meeting thought, it is difficult to claim that Thomas was actually establishing his power. On the other hand, we can argue that he knew his colleagues and was assuming on a rather safe basis what they were probably thinking in the situation. We can also argue that the fact that Thomas himself was feeling that, by being silent he was actually establishing his power is an important sign showing where the power probably was. Did Thomas's successor notice any of this? Probably not! While he might have felt 'powerful' in that moment of mentioning everything that he had achieved and fixed, he was most probably not aware of the whole process unfolding and how the other meeting attendees were feeling.

These two incidents show how silence might redistribute the power cards around the virtual table, at least for a certain time and in a specific situation. In both examples, one could actually argue that the situation might not have been much different face-to-face. This is possible; however, my experience is that precisely because silence gets amplified in the virtual space, particularly when you have cameras off and fewer visual distractors, it is much more noticeable – and who plays with it well, gets noticed!

Sender and receiver: who has power over whom?

Let's now continue in this vein, with what I would describe as a typical situation in the virtual space. Barbara explains:

> For me, virtual meetings are also an important place for 'down time' because I simply do not have enough time to do all my work. In some meetings, I do something else, e.g., I answer my emails or read a document. What would need to happen for me to pay attention? It would need to feel directly relevant, otherwise I switch off and do something else. On the other hand, when I chair a meeting, I expect them to listen to me; I actually check on them and ask them directly. It is arrogant, isn't it? I expect them to pay attention if I am the one chairing the meeting, but I switch off if somebody else does so!

Barbara's reflection clearly raises again the same question of "who has power over whom" in the virtual space. When we are the 'sender', we like to believe that we have the 'power-to' deliver the message that we want to convey and, as mentioned in Proposition 2 (see page 33), we like to believe that we can control whether people are listening to us if we see their face – which is actually an incorrect assumption. As mentioned above, s/he who has the power is actually who decides to listen or not to listen. The virtual space makes a radical shift from 'sender-led' communication to 'receiver-led' communication. Here again, you could argue that also in the face-to-face environment, effective leaders would know that they need to focus on the receiver if they want to have an impact; however, my experience is that leaders with mediocre communication skills will manage somehow to bring their message across face-to-face. They will encounter more quickly and with higher hurdles in the virtual space and get stuck, completely losing their 'power-to', precisely because of the radical shift from 'sender-led' communication to 'receiver-led' communication. In addition, in the virtual space, leaders often fall into the trap of using the same techniques that they would use face-to-face, which as a matter of fact can be disastrous.

Let's take a few examples of techniques used by leaders in virtual meetings. We still have a majority of leaders who hold a presentation in the virtual space in the same way as they would do face-to-face. They expect attendees simply to listen while they go through their thirty minutes of PowerPoint slides. My experience has shown that if one person speaks for longer than four minutes without pausing or at least asking an open question, then attendees will disconnect in the virtual space, no matter how interesting and relevant the content. Instead of conveying content during the meeting (i.e., synchronously when all people are attending together at the same time), leaders should send the content (or their presentation) upfront so that attendees can read them asynchronously (in their own time – see Glossary) and get prepared. That way, meetings focus on discussing and reflecting on the content and on making well-informed decisions. They then become much more engaging and increase the chances for good dialogue. In this case, leaders auto-matically increase their 'power-to' convey the message and discuss it and if real dialogue is achieved this 'power-to' turns into a strong 'power-with', where all feel actively involved and valued and generate good outcomes together.

Another trap is to do precisely what Barbara was mentioning above: *"when I chair a meeting, I expect them to listen to me; I actually check on them and ask them directly"*. What I have learnt throughout many years, is that the worst thing that you can do to a person having an Introvert Preference (see Glossary) is to keep directly asking them questions. These questions will be amplified in their impact virtually and might very soon actually disable attendees with an Introvert Preference to think at the level of depth that they need. As a result, they might either completely withdraw from the conversation or simply say something (that they don't necessarily believe) so that they can be left in peace for a while. In fact, by trying to exercise their 'power-to' through asking questions, leaders might lose completely their 'power-over' those people with an Introvert Preference. Therefore, leaders will need different facilitation skills which will enable them to create the necessary steps for people to step in and speak up if they so wish.

Leaders who know how to bring silence inside out increase their 'power-to' and significantly strengthen their 'power-with'.
Let's now widen the perspective and consider silence in itself, when silence unfolds during a virtual meeting, and nobody speaks. As mentioned earlier, most of the time silence is pregnant with a lot of data. If leaders manage to tap into silence, they will be able to bring deep and often new insights to the surface from their team members. This statement is not only based on my own experience of facilitation throughout the years – it is also based on well-known theories. I would like to mention three key names in this respect. Foulkes (1948, pp. 117–27) developed the concept of 'social unconscious' linked with the theory of a so-called 'matrix'. With 'matrix', he meant the web of unconscious connections that develop between the members of a group when they come together. With 'social unconscious' Foulkes meant the internalised social world that each of us is not aware of, as well as the characteristics of the external world that each of us carries in ourselves without being aware.

Bion (1961, p. 168) expanded the argument that the individual unconscious is not bounded by reality, limitations of time and space and claimed that, as a result, the group unconscious (which I would see as similar to 'social unconscious') also ignores time and space. Weinberg (2014, p. 131) builds on these concepts and shares his wide experience of working with internet groups. He reveals the power of the 'social unconscious' in the virtual space and shows how one can be at the same time physically alone in a room, in front of a computer screen and at the same time completely immersed in the social unconscious of the group that one is joining on the internet. Weinberg (2014, p. 140) writes "[...] we can say that it resides in the potential space between people. The inter-subjective field is a co-creation of the psyche of the people involved in the interaction, meaning that it is not the simple result of the people's unconscious but a new co-unconscious (Moreno, 1934/1978) belonging to neither of the participants". One can find oneself suddenly merging with the unconsciously imagined group, plunging into a role that is infused with projections and introjections – and these phenomena are particularly intensified precisely because they happened in a computer-mediated environment [see Glossary regarding projection and introjection].

At this stage, I ought to mention that Weinberg works mainly with word-based internet groups, where people communicate and interact only with words and not with camera or audio connection. I would nevertheless claim that every aspect mentioned above by Weinberg also applies to group interactions with audio connection. This means that silence in a virtual meeting is an invaluable source of information regarding the team or the group attending the meeting in question, and each individual in the team or group at the same time. When leaders develop the skills to tap into this source of information, they can easily bring to light unspoken and even unconscious aspects of the collaboration. So doing, virtual team dynamics can be explored at a deep level, and this will help the team to move forward and grow.

I would like to share the following example to illustrate the power of tapping into moments of silence in the virtual space. Several years ago, I was training a group of project managers who were leading virtual project teams in the telecommunication industry, across several European countries. During the training, we explored the topic of silence and I taught them several techniques on how to work productively with silence. The key principle was: ***Feel the silence, don't fill it!*** This means that instead of trying to interrupt the silence by asking questions to help the team move forward, one should normalise the silence by saying something like: "I notice the silence and will leave the space on purpose for people to reflect and speak up, if they so wish" – this is important to reassure people that the technical connection is not broken – and then feel one's own intuition in order to sense (rather than think) what this silence might be about. After a while, if nobody speaks up, you share with the team or the group what your intuition tells you: for example, people might be confused about the last part of the conversation, or they might disagree without daring to say it, or they might simply need to take a break. By sharing what your intuition tells you, you are connecting with the meeting attendees at a deeper level, you actually tap into the 'social unconscious'. Sharing what you feel (with your intuition, rather than what you think) will enable somebody else to resonate with it and share as well. So doing, you are 'turning the silence inside-out'. Should your intuition not tell you anything, then after a while, if nobody else speaks up, you might simply ask: "I wonder what this silence tells us?" and invite others to share how the silence feels to them.

At the follow-up session with the group of virtual project managers, one of them, named Frank, shared the following:

> *I cannot believe it. I have been leading this project team for six months now and, while generally speaking the team has been performing at an acceptable level, I have always had the sense that something was not right and is preventing the team from raising the bar. At the last gate-meeting [a key project milestone when team members make the decision whether to proceed to the next phase of product development, for example] we again had one of these situations, where I would ask a question and a wall of silence followed. The question I had asked this time was: "Our project sponsor needs a project report in three days, including the current status of the additional work package that we added last week. Who among you can send him the report? Also, I would like to see it briefly before." This time, instead of thinking: "Here we go again, what is going on, why are they not speaking? I do not see the problem", I decided to experiment and used the techniques learnt at our training. I simply let the silence*

be. After a while, as nobody was speaking, I said: "I do not know about you, but my sense is that we are again stuck somewhere, and I do not know what it is". Then another silence followed and, as I was starting to think "Mmm … not sure what will happen now", one team member, Christina, spoke up: "I do not know what my colleagues think, but I find it increasingly difficult to voice any possible issue in our team. The pace in this project was high from the beginning and it seems to increase by the week, with even more work than the amount we had defined at the kick-off. The way you ask us to deliver makes it very hard for us to voice any potential problem." I was very surprised by what Christina said. She was obviously getting at a blind spot of mine. While I was thinking about the best way to react, somebody else in the team continued saying: "I actually feel the same. There is something in the way we work that makes me feel almost ashamed to say that I cannot cope with the increasing pace". I finally managed to find my words and said: "Thank you! I was not aware of that and I am pleased that you are bringing it up".

Afterwards, a very different type of conversation followed. For the first time it was a genuine conversation about the way we worked together in the team and about my leadership style. I was driving the agenda too much and did not leave any space for people to think and react. I felt as if a stone had been dissolved. Paradoxically, by mentioning my 'stuckness' and letting the silence be, I enabled my team members to speak about their own 'stuckness' and we were able to move on. When I think about it, typically I would have interrupted the silence with several questions about the deadline for the reports, the preliminary steps. I would have offered ways to help them, etc.

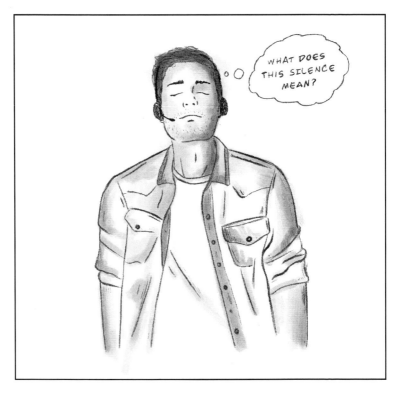

The example on pages 96 and 97 shows how Frank, by working actively and differently with the silence, was able to help his team members to step into their 'power-to' name what was blocking them as a team. This also enabled them to say how Frank's leadership style was almost a taboo for them: they actually valued Frank as team leader very much and therefore found it extremely difficult to speak about his leadership style. In return, by enabling his team members to speak up, Frank himself was strengthening his 'power-with' because, together with the team, they finally had a genuine conversation about the way they wanted to work together. He was also increasing his 'power-to' because he was becoming aware of what he needed to change in his leadership style.

Let silence speak up.
I would like to share a further example from my own practice as virtual facilitator. I was facilitating a virtual team-building

workshop with an executive team of eighteen managers. The team was extremely diverse with twelve nationalities (from several Scandinavian nationalities, to Russian, Czech, French, German, Austrian, Dutch, Indian and Chinese). The team was not only diverse in terms of nationalities but in terms of professions, levels of experience, and also in terms of their understanding about what the team's purpose should be. The team had been struggling with their diversity and was genuinely seeking ways to turn this liability into an asset, exploring how they could turn this diversity into something that would increase their performance.

During the workshop, the team worked to define a team charter in order to improve their performance in the virtual space. Tacitly they all knew that there were some tensions in the team and every time I invited the team to explore these, a few strong characters in the team would take over the discussion and claim that there were no particular tensions and that if there were any, these would be absolutely normal given the high level of diversity in and the large size of the team. Their view was that the team simply needed to take the situation as it was and should focus on the challenging tasks at hand. I knew that this was only one view in the team, supported by a few. I also knew that many others did not share that view. For some reason they did not want to speak up. At one point the discussion became silent, which had not happened a lot so far in the workshop. I took the opportunity to give this silence more space by saying: "I notice the silence and would like to invite you to use this space to check where you all are in the process." Then a long silence developed, and all my senses were actually clearly identifying a strong disagreement and discomfort in the team. At some point, having let the silence be for quite a while, I intervened: "I wonder how you interpret this silence. My intuition tells me that there is a strong disagreement in the team". Immediately after this, one of the strong characters said that they did not feel this disagreement and that we should move on. At which point, one of the silent participants, who disagreed with the view that there were no tensions, spoke up and said to the person wanting to move on: "Actually, there is a conversation that we should have and that we always avoid … Just the way you said that tensions in our team were not a real issue makes me feel 'stupid', with my own perception that they actually are an issue".

Another person then joined in and said: "The problem is that every time I try to say that we have a problem, I get a swift reaction from some of you like 'Why are you always so negative? You should look at what works, before looking at what does not work'. I feel judged and not safe to express an opinion, which I think is only my opinion and I feel left alone with it." After that, three more people carried on, building on each other, and expressing that they felt that there was no place nor any time in the team to voice their diversity in such a way that others would embrace it. We then moved on and the team worked on ways to leave space for their diversity and to voice tensions and disagreement in a manner that others could hear without judgement. The team looked at the typical sentences that they would say to each other which would shut colleagues up because of the way they were framed and voiced. They made a table, which listed on the one side: "What we do not want to say to each other any longer" and on the other side: "What we want to say instead". The iceberg had been dissolved, if not completely, at least to a reasonable level of depth in a way that the team could now have the conversations that they needed to have. And this with the full support and encouragement of their leader.

This example shows again the power of letting the silence be. Actually, here it was almost like creating space through facilitation to let the silence unfold. The silence was turned inside out by having more and more team members speaking up and voicing something that had become a real hurdle to their virtual collaboration. By enabling several people to speak up and increase their 'power-to' name something that was slowing them down in a way that could not be turned down any longer, they became able to develop a strong 'power-with', enabling them to redefine ways of communicating and working differently with each other.

TO SUMMARISE

Silence, if used with high levels of self-awareness and process-awareness, can be a significant source of power. Silence can help leaders to protect their own power. Silence can also be a very effective vehicle to enable others to step into their power and speak up. It can also be a very impactful way of bringing deep, unspoken dynamics of virtual teams out on to the virtual table.

IMPLICATIONS FOR LEADERS

Leaders need to realise that silence is a good thing. They should not try to break it with questions or statements, they should explore it using their intuition: ***FEEL the silence, don't FILL it!***

Leaders should also normalise the silence and help their team members to acknowledge it as an important part of a virtual conversation.

Leaders are invited to develop the skills to tap into silence and bring the silence 'inside out' by enabling others to speak about it. So doing they will significantly increase their 'power-with' and enable their team to grow.

CHAPTER 12 –
Proposition 7: When the human body gets in the way – The virtual space neutralises gender differences and titles

Power differentials between genders are different in the virtual space and can be more easily neutralised to offer a level playing field for all. This in turn has significant implications for the strategic agendas of diversity and inclusion in corporations and public organisations.

The question of how gendered power differentials would play out in a virtual environment emerged differently from all the previous questions in our research project. It did not emerge from any co-researchers' personal experiences, but instead because of the strong focus they were putting on diversity and inclusion. They therefore chose to direct attention towards observing the effects of gender in the context of the virtual leadership and collaboration practices within their respective organisations.

Gendered power differentials can be strong in traditional leadership.
Buchanan and Badham (2008, p. 30) summarise a vast amount of research being done about the different approaches to power of women and men in the traditional paradigm. They come to the general conclusion that, in most cases, women do not want to play organisational politics. They explain how many women reject management roles because of their distaste for political behaviour. They mention gender stereotypes, such as women being seen as 'politically innocent and naïve', 'emphasising rapport and "we" in their communication', 'using formal systems [as opposed to informal networks] to get information', to name a few (p. 159). They also

underline the importance of impression management as a way to increase one's own personal power: "Impression management is the process by which we control the image that others have of us. [...] Effective impression management means being aware of and in control of the cues that we send to others through verbal and non-verbal channels. In these ways, we consciously manipulate the perceptions that others have of us, and therefore shape their behaviour, too. [...] The more effectively we manage our impression, [...] the greater our ability to achieve our preferred outcomes" (p. 60).

Eagly and Karau (2002) and (2007) take a slightly different, although in my view complementary, stance. They explain that prescriptive gender behaviours are incompatible with conventional leader roles and, therefore, females are disadvantaged with respect to assuming leadership positions. By wanting to reach power in an organisation, women have to display what we might call 'male' behaviours that differ from the female stereotypes. If they do display these behaviours, they would most likely be disliked: "Thus, individuals who display deviant gender stereotypic behaviours may face resistance or be evaluated negatively by their peers or supervisors" (2002, p. 592). I would like to underline that these two views are related to the traditional, mainly face-to-face-based, leadership paradigm.

The power of the new COO in the virtual environment

In contrast, I would like to share the emerging findings from our research about gender-based power differentials in the virtual paradigm. Let's take a concrete example brought up by Steve:

> *Last year I joined a meeting with our new COO. The meeting was virtual and included all members of the executive team. During the meeting, she presented a few KPIs and then engaged in a discussion with us. She made an impression on me of being confident, articulate, knowing what she was talking about, task focused while at the same time paying attention to all of us in the team. We were all men apart from her. A few weeks afterwards I had the opportunity to meet her face-to-face. She was petite and more reserved. I must admit that I did not picture her like that at all in our virtual meeting!*

The most interesting part of this example is the fact that the picture Steve developed from the new COO virtually was different from the picture that he got when seeing her face-to-face. Did the fact that she was 'confident', 'articulate' and 'knowing her stuff' lead Steve to assume that she was taller or, vice versa: Did the fact that she was, as a matter of fact, 'petite' lead Steve to revisit his opinion of her? Steve did not actually say that he was revisiting his opinion of her, simply that he was very surprised by the physical appearance of the new COO. Would the situation have been the same if the new COO had been a man?

Oh Peter, I thought you were much taller!

Let me share a further example to contrast the previous one. Many years ago, I was asked by the leader of a global services team to train the team to become a high-performing virtual team. The Danish global company that they belonged to had completely restructured the organisation and the team had become responsible for delivering global services such as finance, reporting, IT, etc. to the whole organisation worldwide. They needed to hit the ground running. There were eleven team members, distributed around the globe. Many of them had never met face-to-face; the same applied to me as their trainer. We engaged in a virtual workshop delivered on three consecutive days, followed by a series of four follow-up sessions during which they would report their individual progress in the implementation of the new strategy, supporting and challenging each other to master the issues at hand. In the group, there was an Indian person that I will call Peter to protect his identity. From the very beginning, Peter was engaged, poised, very focused and fast at understanding the issues discussed. In his gentle, yet authoritative way he would be very helpful to his peers, while at the same time open about his own challenges. Peter would often be the one to bring an excellent question or a strong insight. Even if all of them (apart from the leader) were peers, one could feel seniority and wisdom in Peter's presence. Just before the last follow-up session, the team leader asked me whether I would be willing to facilitate a strategy conference face-to-face in Spain for his whole function with approximately fifty managers. This was a different assignment, unrelated to the virtual leadership training that I had with his global services team. I mentioned this to the global services team at our final session and we started mentally playing with the idea of standing in front of each other face-to-face, after having worked intensively with each other in the virtual space over a period of six months. The curiosity, paired with a light apprehension, was justified because we, on purpose, did not use cameras for our virtual-team-building training and, as mentioned before, while a few team members had met face-to-face, many others had not. The maximum that they would have had was a picture of each other on the intranet; as a matter of fact, this incident took place in 2007, well before the implementation of tools such as MS Teams or Skype.

As soon as I arrived in the conference room in Spain, I started checking the settings and logistics. Participants were slowly arriving. I wondered whether and how quickly I would recognise the members of the global services team. I did not have to wonder long, because very soon six of the team members were gathered around me. For them, it was easy to recognise me because they knew that there would be only two ladies in the group: one Asian colleague and myself. I (as a European) was therefore easy to recognise. At some point, we had nine of the global services team members gathered with me in the room. Peter had just joined. He was easy to recognise because of his Indian traits (he was the only Asian male in the global services team). As soon as Peter greeted everybody, one of his Danish colleagues (that I will call Gerry) very spontaneously said: "Oh, Peter, I thought you were much taller!". Many burst out laughing in a kind way. Peter was indeed rather small.

This story shows how Peter's strong, helpful and assertive presence in the virtual space had led Gerry to develop the picture of him as a tall man. Here again, we have the situation of specific stereotypes attributed to specific behaviours and character traits. Were Peter's peers now considering him as less competent, less strong or less assertive because of his small size? Probably not, but at first, they were for sure pretty disconcerted by his embodied appearance to say the least.

This example shows the phenomenon that I would call 'when the human body gets in the way'. This phenomenon is not necessarily linked to a gender question. It is more linked to stereotypes that we might have in our minds. It is also a clear sign that many people still seem to privilege the physical appearance as a point of reference in order to develop a sense of a person, rather than their behaviour, competences, values and character.

Nevertheless, this issue of power differentials in the virtual space is more complicated than that. I would like to offer another personal example to illustrate my statement.

When human body gets in the way

Ten years ago, I was still active as a tutor in traditional leadership development for middle to senior managers of different global organisations. At the business school I was working for, we used to work in tandem, i.e., two tutors in groups of up to forty people. One of the people I worked with on a regular basis was Colin. Colin is a very experienced tutor with very effective teaching approaches; he is a likeable person that participants would very quickly learn to value a lot. Colin is a tall and slim man. I myself am rather petite. Our teaching styles were very different from each other, and clients would particularly appreciate the way we complemented each other. At some point, with the rise of global virtual teams, I was asked by one of our clients, a global German company, to deliver a leadership development program for their most senior leaders as a series of four modules, with one of them in the middle being delivered virtually and dedicated to virtual leadership. The programs went very well. Colin and I enjoyed a lot the interactions with these leaders, which became more open, authentic and spontaneous from module to module. In one of the programs, as I was carrying out small focus groups to prepare for one of the upcoming modules, I suddenly got the very unexpected and certainly unprompted feedback from two of the leaders: "Ghislaine, I must say that I am impressed by your presence in the virtual space. Your power is much stronger than face-to-face. You come across as so much more assertive. You really know what you are talking about". His colleague echoed the same: "I was also surprised by how differently you came across to me. You were so authoritative and confident". It took me some time to reflect on this feedback and I came to the conclusion: well, my body must be getting in the way!

One wonders: was it the same phenomenon as that which happened to Peter? Or was it more about the power differentials between genders? Or was it both? My personal example is the same story– albeit the other way round – as the one of the new COO in Steve's company: the new COO first met her colleagues of the executive team virtually, and then face-to-face and I met the partici-pants first face-to-face and then virtually. In both cases however, like in Peter's case, there was a readjustment needed between the picture one had from the person face-to-face and the picture one had of the person virtually. What we can say for sure is that the virtual space seems to neutralise the effects that stereotypes might have on the way one perceives a person. One stereotype would be that a person who is competent, self-confident, and assertive has to be tall. Another stereotype would be that a petite woman (in the eyes of some people: one physical trait particularly emphasising one aspect of the female gender) has to be, by definition, less strong and assertive. It also seems that this phenomenon 'when the human body gets in the way' particularly happens regarding gender differences. However, I believe that more research is required in order to confirm this.

The following view of Norman in our inquiry group seems to confirm the above though:

> *There is a gender neutralisation in the virtual space. If meetings are well facilitated, the difference goes to the minimum: only the voice makes a difference. In face-to-face we predominantly have the 'testosterone' effect. In my environment, there is a strong male focus. In our management meetings, we only have one lady in the room, and she remains silent. In the digital meetings, everyone has a voice. She speaks up, like any of us. Also, when we join into the virtual meeting, the attendees' names are listed depending on the sequence when people join, not according to their status and this makes a difference* [Norman refers here to the vertical list of names on the virtual collaboration platform].

Norman's view is echoed very strongly in the wider research. Tom Tong and Walther (2015, p. 205) claim: "In CMC [computer mediated communication], the control over verbal cues and messages is a distinct advantage: Although less information is being transmitted through linguistic cues than through multimodal channels, this information is more controllable, allowing communicators to effect their interactional goals."

Some very interesting and important research findings are shared by Yong-Kwan Lim, Chidambaram and Carte (2008, p. 5). They look at emerging leaders in virtual teams. With 'emerging' leaders, they mean leaders who exert influence on others, but are not necessarily formally appointed as leaders. In other words, they investigated leaders who would step into their leadership in specific moments of a project, for example. They claim the following: "... we argue that such technologies [computer meditated technology] offer a more level playing field for minority members, i.e., females. As such, we discuss the idea that, in a setting characterised by a high degree of reductive capabilities, females are not as obligated to engage in impression management strategies that are in line with femininity and are free to break away from gender stereotypes."

In addition, Yong-Kwan Lim et al. explain regarding asynchronous meetings that the technology, precisely when it is asynchronous in the communication, reduces the 'normal turn taking' of a conversation that would often take place in a face-to-face setting. Hence, the interruption tactics that according to Buchanan and Badham (2008, p. 61) are often used to assert one's own power in face-to-face automatically get neutralised in the virtual space. In asynchronous virtual meetings, any individual can post their messages on the platform at any time. Further, even in synchronous virtual meetings, each individual can send their message to others without interruptions – for example via the chat room. Yong-Kwan Lim et al. go as far as to claim that, as such, the use of synchronous or asynchronous meetings reduces monopolisation of conversations by dominant members and permits greater equality of participation.

At this stage, I would like to underline an example brought up by Jade, which echoes the findings mentioned above. She explains that, during global virtual meetings in her organisation, she often needs to encourage the African women to speak up. Usually, the African men would speak first, and the African women would be quiet and remain so, unless actively asked to speak up by Jade. The interesting and important difference though is that, in this situation, the African team (i.e., women and men) would sit in the same physical room and join the international teleconference. In other words, the power dynamics described here are more the ones from a face-to-face environment, even if the African team would be linked in virtually with the rest of the team members around the organisation. When the degree of virtuality is higher, for example in the asynchronous strategy conference that I facilitated for the same organisation, then the same African women, like any other participants, would actively contribute and speak up via the posts that they would write on the platform.

The above suggests that the virtual space neutralises power differentials or at least significantly changes the rules of the game for minorities of all types, particularly – but not exclusively – for female leaders.

Titles and 'labels' play a less important role virtually.
At this point, I want to expand the scope beyond gender differences and focus on the general phenomenon of 'labels' and how these operate in the virtual compared with the face-to-face environment.

Reitz and Higgins (2019, pp. 84–100) clearly underline that the use and awareness of titles (e.g., director, president, etc.) and 'labels' in a wider sense (e.g., woman/man, young/old, outsider/insider, people of colour, etc.) have a major impact on the readiness of managers to speak up and/or to listen to others who speak up. What they say, independently of how competent and relevant it is, is automatically filtered and seen as more 'true' or less 'true', depending on the titles and labels that they carry and on what the listener is associating with those.

Lynn, one of our co-researchers explains: *"In virtual collaboration, when I do not know the background and the titles, I feel more courageous. If I do know the titles, I am more reserved with my own opinion. It is interesting that face-to-face we would exchange business cards first as a ritual".*

I personally find that aspect highly important. The face-to-face ritual of exchanging business cards across the table does assert everyone's status and title. My experience is that virtually, if the meeting is well facilitated and the focus is set on establishing the human connection rather than the status at the start, then the impact is different and the 'titles' and/or 'labels' play a significantly limited role. Often, only the attendees' names are listed on the right-hand side of the meeting platform and titles or status, even if briefly mentioned, do not seem to 'stick' very long in the attendees' minds.

Marcus, another co-researcher shared something similar: *"When you start the discussion with people that you do not know (you do not know their title and function) you are open, and you discuss in depth. But if you see the face on the camera or if you know the title, then you might be more guarded instead of sharing your real opinion. This is especially true when the power distance is strong, particularly in Asian cultures".*

It is more difficult to recover from bad first impressions virtually than face-to-face.

More than the titles and labels, the first impressions that managers make, for example when they join a new team or even when they join a cross-functional meeting, seem to matter much more in virtual collaboration. My experience is that these first impressions are much longer lasting than face-to-face. For example, if a person joins a meeting late, or if they are equipped with a bad quality audio-system, the other attendees will remember that person for some time as "the one who was not audible" or the "one who was late", etc. It is more difficult to recover from unhelpful first impressions virtually than face-to-face. Yong-Kwan Lim et al (2008, p. 21) claim: "Once impressions are formed, they are unlikely to change in the short term. They may change over the longer term, as groups build a history of interactions and performance, but those changes are likely to be slow".

Compared to the impression management in the face-to-face environment mentioned above, successful impression management in the virtual space is different. Aspects such as expertise and knowledge (see page 76) are more likely to help managers establish their leadership.

Finally, I would like to add a few remarks related to voice. While it seems that face-to-face, the use of a lower voice register and speaking more slowly are seen as strategies for managers to establish their power (Buchanan and Badham, 2008, p. 61), we did not reach any conclusive results related to voice in the virtual space, apart from the obvious need to pay attention to clear pronunciation and articulation. In my experience, women also ought to pay attention to the pitch of their voice, which should not be too high, precisely because the degree of 'stridence' will get amplified virtually and become unpleasant to others' ears. In the same way, men ought to pay attention if their voice is too low in the voice register, because it might be difficult for others to hear them well. Also, their speech might quickly become monotonous, which will lead others to lose focus and disengage. These are however more learning points from my own experience and based on my work in the last nineteen years with many leaders in the virtual space. The most important point is that leaders ought to regularly record themselves and check their voice to ensure that they integrate this essential part of their personality into the awareness of their own presence in the virtual space. I will expand on this in Chapter 13.

The whole topic of neutralisation of power differentials in virtual environments certainly deserves more research. However, based on the findings presented above, I am confident that we can point out the following implications, which are summarised below:

TO SUMMARISE

Computer-mediated environments allow women to break out of gender-stereotypical impression management strategies and establish themselves as leaders without facing potential backlashes if their behaviours do not correspond to their gender stereotypes, which is what generally happens in face-to-face settings.

Any individual can free themselves from stereotypes associated with specific physical traits and be perceived as competent, leaderful etc. independent of or despite their physical appearance. Their expertise, behaviours, values, etc. will be recognised as such and they will be able to step into their 'power-to', precisely because their body will not get in the way.

Computer-mediated environments can also neutralise the impact of 'titles' and 'labels' and therefore people might be more prone to speak up and to step into their 'power-to'.

IMPLICATIONS FOR VIRTUAL LEADERS

Leaders and managers should consider using more asynchronous meeting platforms, particularly at the beginning of a project or in the context of strategy or innovation initiatives because a more level playing field will be created for women and people who might become victims of stereotypes because of their physical appearance. This will enable those who are victims of stereotypes to step into their 'power-to' by focusing on the task and the expertise at hand.

CHAPTER 13 –
Powerful in the virtual space – recapitulation and recommendations

This final chapter recapitulates what managers and leaders can do to be 'powerful' whilst also enabling others to step into their power in the virtual space. The research reported in this book shows that power works differently in the virtual space. In many aspects, developing power - in oneself, in other people, and in the team - is different in the virtual world compared to the face-to-face environment.

Many of the recommendations in this chapter can be implemented straight away and form a key part of creating a culture of speaking up in the virtual space. Here, leaders and managers are invited to learn – and to unlearn – what it takes to fulfil the potential for collaborating and leading in the virtual space. This means letting go of some taken-for-granted strategies so as to avoid falling into difficult traps.

The chapter is in two parts: first, what can leaders and managers do to develop a culture of speaking up in virtual meetings? And second, what can leaders and managers do to increase their own power in the virtual space?

1. What leaders can do to develop a culture of speaking up

No mix of face-to-face and virtual!
As mentioned in Proposition 1, I would like to strongly encourage leaders and managers to avoid virtual meetings of any type (whether these are regular meetings or conferences or workshops) where

some people are connected virtually, and others are sitting together in the same physical space. This creates power differentials that can be disruptive and can silence people. The particular difficulty is that this phenomenon does not get openly spoken about for the reasons mentioned in Chapter 6 and soon becomes a taboo. Unfortunately, this situation is current practice in several organisations, even more so in hybrid teams. Challenging this status quo might feel daunting at times. It will require courage and determination as well as change management skills. Rather than imposing this practice on their teams, leaders and managers will need to be transparent about the need to change, explain the reasons and engage their team members in an experiment, so that all can experience the difference when they are all in separate environments and can reflect about the advantages of this – even if this practice might feel odd and counter-intuitive at first. Obviously, implementing this practice might have logistical implications in some organisations and many might first think: it is not possible to do this, we have an open plan office! For those, I refer to the practical tips that I provide in Chapter 6, page 31.

I would also like to invite team coaches, OD consultants and executive coaches to challenge managers' and leaders' views regarding the practice of mixed connections in virtual meetings. I have heard a few times: "Well, we did have our workshop in a mixed-mode because the client would not accept anything else, and it worked!" Of course, it will work up to a certain level. But, as mentioned in Chapter 6 and underlined above, the topic of mixed-meetings is often a taboo. Hence, while attendees might not challenge the status quo, at the same time they might withdraw from speaking up if they are the ones connected virtually. As with leaders and managers, I would like to invite coaches and OD consultants to challenge the status quo. Even though it might feel difficult, it is worth doing as this will enable a real culture of dialogue to flourish in the virtual space.

No cameras!
I have demonstrated in Chapter 7 and Chapter 12 how not using cameras and, more generally, how a meeting mode with rather fewer communication channels (e.g., word only or word and audio) can

promote a more egalitarian environment and encourage all to speak their truth and to step into their power. When people do not use cameras, they might be more likely to be in touch with their own selves, with their own beliefs and opinions and be more prone to express these because they will be less distracted and less influenced by the body language and facial expressions of others. Not using cameras will help team members to be less fearful and speak up, even if their opinion might not be the same as the majority. This exchange will need to be well facilitated though, and robust psychological safety rules need to be established from the outset.

Become a communication designer!
In Chapter 8 and Chapter 12, I explain how leaders and managers need to make conscious decisions about the type of technology that they use for their virtual collaboration and leadership. Obviously, they might not be completely free to decide by themselves as many organisations have IT departments that prescribe the technology platforms to use, looking at important criteria such as security and costs. In the cases where managers and leaders cannot choose the technology platforms themselves, they can at least decide how to work with them. They will need to learn about the features of these platforms and the impact these will have on the behaviours of their team members. Rather than letting themselves be led by technology, which in itself, as demonstrated in Chapter 8, has implicitly embedded traditional forms of hierarchical power in its very structure, they need to become masters of technology and what I would call 'communication designers'. They do not need to be technical experts though! For example, by choosing to use more asynchronous communication platforms (in addition to not using cameras), they will create a more level playing field for all involved and automatically raise levels of inclusivity, also in teams with high diversity levels. By choosing not to use the mute button, emoticons and symbols like 'raise hand' and promoting spontaneity in the virtual exchange instead, they will foster a real culture of dialogue in the virtual space. This means that leaders and managers need to be choiceful about which technology they use and how they use it. **They need to lead the use of technology instead of being led by it.** In the same way as they would plan their meeting with the

corresponding agenda, list of attendees and material to support decision-making, they will also need to plan or, better still, carefully design the communication processes and choose the corresponding features to support these.

It also means that they will need to consciously **work against the traditional digital etiquette** that has established itself over the years as a result of an implicit, automatic transfer from face-to-face meeting habits on to the virtual space. I mentioned and elaborated on the key aspects of this on pages 46 and 47. Therefore, I will only summarise them here: encourage people to interrupt, encourage people not to say their name before they speak (once they have introduced themselves), encourage people to 'nod' virtually when they support each other's opinion and encourage them not to mute, so that they can be spontaneous, interrupt and nod at any moment*. At this stage, I would like to reiterate an important point: when I claim that virtual leaders should encourage their team members to interrupt each other, the kind of 'interrupting' that I advocate has a very different quality from the 'interrupting' mentioned on page 47, referring to the tactics of some leaders who want to state their power in the face-to-face environment as claimed by Buchanan and Badham (2010). The 'interrupting' that I mean here is one of being constantly in the flow of the conversation and interrupting at the right moment, for example by asking a question, adding an important aspect to the theme at hand or nodding to support what is being discussed, etc. I do not mean 'interrupting' to actually stop the flow of a conversation by bringing a counter argument or simply making one's own new point.

Be prepared to challenge upwards and speak up!
In Chapter 8, I have illustrated the difficulty of collaborating and leading virtually people who do not know what they don't know – people who simply transfer on to the virtual environment the way they would collaborate and lead face-to-face because they have not recognised yet that the virtual space is a different paradigm. This

---

* For more tips about how to create an engaging meeting culture, please look at our videos "14 Tips for effective virtual meetings" on: https://www.black-gazelle.com/index.php?option=com_content&view=article&id=42/&It emid=264

might create a real dilemma among those who know what they know (about the virtual environment as a different paradigm) as to whether they should challenge their hierarchy or not if the people in question are their superiors. It is not always easy to challenge one's own boss and tell them that they have to unlearn and learn anew how to collaborate and lead virtually. Particularly in organisations with strong hierarchy, this might feel daunting, if not risky. And yet, the price of not doing it will be high: managers and leaders who will have developed virtual leadership and collaboration competences will become more and more frustrated and the performance of the organisation will remain 'second class', or inferior to face-to-face collaboration, if they regularly get stopped in their efforts to raise the bar of virtual collaboration by their superiors. Organisations might quickly get stuck at a certain level of virtual collaboration and even develop cynicism about that. I would like to encourage leaders and managers who know what they know about the virtual paradigm of collaboration and leadership to engage in one-to-one conversations with their superiors (these can also be peers of course) and make them aware of the pitfalls of transferring on to the virtual space collaboration and leadership habits from the face-to-face paradigm.

I would also like to strongly encourage managers and heads of Human Resources in organisations to take a proactive leadership role in this cultural change in their company's collaboration culture instead of simply letting things emerge. More practical tips on how to achieve this can be found on pages 61 and 62.

Before moving on to summarising what leaders and managers can do to increase their own 'power-to', I would like to conclude these considerations about what leaders and managers can do to enable their team to speak up with the following: implementing the actions and approaches described above will go beyond the sheer virtual collaboration and virtual leadership of an organisation. It will actually change the company culture at its very core, because it will migrate from a traditional face-to-face paradigm into the virtual paradigm. It will require courage and a systematic approach, based on dialogue and learning.

2. What leaders can do to increase their own 'power-to'

Leaders and managers have a real choice and a chance to increase their 'power-to'. There are several things that they can do. Some require a different attitude, some require specific skills and some require a strengthened awareness of themselves and others around them.

Invite on to your platform!

The first thing that I would encourage you to do, building on the findings shared in Chapter 8, is to make sure that you are the one inviting people on to 'your' meeting platform. In other words, if you can be the one choosing the platform and the features and deciding how you want to use them to achieve the outcomes that you wish to achieve, then you will have a much better chance to increase your 'power-to'. As I have explained in Chapter 8 and reiterated above, technology platforms and features can have a strong impact on the collaboration culture of your team(s). This will be particularly important if you work with external parties; by inviting them to 'your' virtual platform, you are inviting them to 'your' office so to speak, and definitely to your world of virtual collaboration. So doing, you will more easily step into your 'power-to'.

Knowledge and expertise are significant sources of power in the virtual space.

As explained in Chapter 9, knowledge and expertise potentially have a much higher impact on your 'power-to' in the virtual space. It is therefore important that you prepare yourself well and that you ensure the quality of data that you present (the likelihood that mistakes or errors get noticed in the virtual space is much higher than face-to-face). It is also essential to make conscious decisions on how you present your knowledge or expertise. The typical PowerPoint presentations held face-to-face are to be avoided; conveying data or input of any type ought to be done asynchronously, so that during the meetings the time can be used for interactive exchange and sense-making, when you can guide the reflection of your peers or of your team members on the basis of your knowledge or expertise. I might remind you of the simple tip:

avoid speaking for longer than four minutes without pausing or asking a question. This will help you to keep people engaged and increase your 'power-to' influence them.

See communication as ACTION with power – not as power in action!

Be aware that communication goes far beyond transfer of information; it is ACTION! Communication is actually action in two ways.

With your choice of words, you can take action and lead others to do the same. As explained in Chapter 10, this requires a different language from the language that you might have been using face-to-face. Particularly if you work in global virtual teams or in teams with high levels of diversity, it is essential that you use straight, direct and yet respectful language. Avoid "We ought to ..." if you actually mean "You should ...". Avoid "I would prefer this approach" if you mean "Please take this approach instead". Straight language (as often believed by English native speakers for example) does not have to be rude or confrontational or impolite; it can be respectful and very effective, particularly when communicating with non-native speakers. The same applies to situations when you work with team members reporting to you in the so-called dotted line in a matrix organisation and also with peers or even with external parties that you need to influence.

Furthermore, if you notice that you are not achieving what you would like to achieve with a certain person, instead of doing more of the same (for example by providing more information or by asking the same questions), demonstrate greater empathy and do make a real effort to develop a good understanding of what and how the message that you sent virtually is actually being received. Everything gets amplified virtually; hence, if you keep asking the same good old open questions for example, you might quickly 'freeze' the communication because, in the virtual space, too many open questions in a row get significantly sharper than in face-to-face and actually block your counterpart. If you keep sending even more information, you might soon lose the recipient's attention. Demonstrate versatility and heightened empathy instead; and this is also ACTION, which can at times feel like hard work. Practising heightened empathy will in turn require different skills from face-to-face. Many managers have been trained in the so-called concept of 'active listening', which often equates to listening so that you can ask the next good question, potentially in the hope of leading your counterpart on to the path that you were hoping they would take. Listening in the virtual space should be **listening to actually understand** in a holistic way, by remaining sufficiently silent, noticing what is being said and what is not being said and working with one's own intuition. In other words, it means learning to read the different layers of voice to really understand what your counterpart is thinking and feeling.

Much more than face-to-face, virtual communication requires more precision, more succinctness and more empathy, achieved through better and different listening. Managers who develop the necessary skills to achieve this, will significantly increase their 'power-to'.

Please mind the grip!
As I explored extensively in Chapter 7 and reiterated above, not using cameras can actually significantly increase managers' 'power-to' and make them less fearful to speak up. Nevertheless, as demonstrated with the several Critical Incidents, it is essential that managers quickly and accurately recognise whether they speak up from a place of true connectivity with the team and the unfolding conversation (being in the flow), as opposed to a place of high sensitivity to triggers in the conversation that might 'press their buttons' and lead them to react with strong unhelpful emotions (being in the grip). When managers are in the flow, as seen in Chapter 7, they enable others to step into their 'power-to' and, in so doing, increase their 'power-with'. When managers are in the grip, they actually cut others off from their power and lose their own 'power-to', because as we have seen in the many examples explored, they actually end up facing a wall of silence and damaging working relationships, at least for a while.

Recognising when you are in the grip, as opposed to in the flow, requires heightened self-awareness, robust process-awareness as well as a discipline of mindfulness, for example through the practice of a 'focus exercise' (see an example of a focus exercise referred to in 15.3 in the Appendix) before your virtual meeting as a way to avoid projections and introjections (also see Glossary).

Feel the silence, don't fill it!

As explained in Chapter 11, managers and leaders who learn how to work well with silence will be able to increase their 'power-to' and as a result their 'power-with' their teams. Silence is an inherent part of every conversation; while one minute of silence might be comfortably experienced face-to-face, it might feel like five minutes in the virtual space. For some managers and leaders, silence might soon become a real challenge virtually and their natural temptation is often to interrupt silence by asking further questions and/or making statements in order to move on. In other words, *they tend to fill silence* with questions and statements. This equates to a significant lost opportunity because silence is pregnant with important information.

Silence often bears the so-called 'social unconscious' (see page 94) of a team. Knowing how to skillfully tap into this silence will enable managers and leaders to make explicit essential implicit knowledge, beliefs, values, etc. which might hold a team back. Making those explicit, and enabling team members to speak about them, might have a releasing, almost therapeutic effect. At the very least, it will make team members aware of them and take action on them. So doing, team members learn to free themselves from unconscious barriers and to step into their 'power-to' speak up. As a result, team maturity grows, and leaders increase their 'power-with' the team. To achieve this, leaders need to take a specific approach: first normalise the silence for all (so that people can relax into it instead of wondering whether they have lost the technical connection), hold the silence long enough, use their intuition *to feel the silence* and what it might be bearing and then share what their sense of the silence is (as opposed to asking people why they are silent), so that they enable others to share their own sense of silence as well. By doing this step-by-step and with care, they are, so to say, *turning silence inside out*, as opposed to closing it and moving on. It is about letting silence speak up and voicing the team's unconscious.

Become friends with your voice!

I am still surprised by how few managers and leaders ever ask themselves about the image that their voice is projecting about their presence in the virtual space. Instead of being focused on face-to-face tactics supposed to increase their 'power-to', such as speaking within a lower register or speaking slowly (see page 112), managers and leaders should put their energy into two essentials. First, they should ensure that the quality of their communication logistics (internet line and quality of their audio connection) is excellent. I often meet with managers who, when confronted with the fact that they are hard to hear in the virtual space because of bad equipment, have nothing better to say than: "But I can hear everybody very well!" Paying attention to your audio equipment when you attend or lead a virtual meeting is like making a conscious choice of the clothes that you want to wear when you meet face-to-face. Your audio connection is your virtual business card! Second, managers and leaders should regularly record themselves in order to integrate the awareness of their voice as an inherent and essential part of their identity. Often managers and leaders tell me: "I hate listening to my voice. I sound horrible". The fact that we do not hear ourselves in the same way as others do is due to our physiology and it is therefore particularly important that we know how others hear us if we want to maximise our impact on others and increase our 'power-to'. In this effort, before judging your voice, it is important to embrace it as it is, to *become friends with your voice*, because this is the voice that has served you so far and you ought to integrate the awareness of this 'friend' into your own sense of identity. Once you have become friends with your voice, you might want to consider the following aspects: the pitch of your voice, the degree of articulation (how clear and how sustained it is), the colour of your voice (is it bright or dark) and the level of variation or monotony that you might notice in your intonation, pitch and speed of speech. It is then up to you – and you alone – to decide what you might wish to change – or whether you wish to change anything at all. **Stay away from voice engineering and cultivate voice awareness instead!**

CHAPTER 14 –
Closing remarks

Coming to the end of writing this book, I wonder how you, the reader, might feel when you come to the end of reading it. Do you feel confirmed in what you know and practise, excited at the prospect of applying some of the approaches, sceptical, daunted?

Some of the recommendations might indeed feel daunting as they require much higher levels of awareness, competences and skills than in the face-to-face. Simply put, leading in the virtual space obliges you to become a better leader. As everything gets amplified virtually, more precision and deeper awareness are needed. I hope that you will be up for riding these waves of challenges; experimenting and learning from it can feel exhilarating in your 'power-to' and 'power-with' and will certainly make a difference in how you enable others to step into their power in the virtual space.

Should some of the propositions feel too daunting or simply too challenging for you, I would like to invite you to start with the ones that resonate the most and to experiment with these first. When you start harvesting the fruits of your efforts, you can always come back to the book and experiment with some of the remaining ones.

While I feel confident that the propositions presented in this book are robust and valid, I would also encourage others to keep inquiring and experimenting with them, alongside additional ones that might emerge, as they may reveal even more potential to enrich our understanding of power dynamics in the virtual space. The journey has only started and, as Daniel Timms shares in the Sheffield Tribune of 1st March 2022: "We overestimate the impact of a technology in the short-run but underestimate it in the long run."

Finally, I would also like to put this reflection on power in the virtual space in a wider perspective. The American Parker Follet

(1868–1933), pioneer of management theories, wrote: "That is always our problem, not how to get control of people, but how all together we can get control of a situation" (Melé and Rosanas 2003, p.38). I believe that her words are truer than ever.

CHAPTER 15 – Appendix

15.1 Details about my co-researchers

Anna, German, social media and PR Director, works for a German company in the chemical industry

Audrey, German, based in Germany, Global OD Manager in a global German company in automotive

Barbara, British, CEO of a global NGO dealing with children in poverty

Jade, Finnish, CEO of a global NGO dealing with alcohol and drug addiction

Jeff, French, Global Director for Production, works for a global Swedish company in the medical sector

Jo, Chinese, based in Singapore, Head of Marketing works for a global Swedish company in the medical sector

John, German, Vice President, Global Logistics, works for a global German company in automotive

Julia, Australian, Project Leader Global Research, works for a global Foundation with Headquarters in Austria

Lynn, Singaporean, based in Asia Pacific, Director HR of a global Swedish company in the medical sector

Marcus, Chinese, Head of Logistics working for a global German company in automotive

Matthew, British, Research Manager, working for a global health organisation

Norman, Egyptian, General Manager based in UAE, works for a Danish global company in the medical sector

Patricia, British, responsible for OD in a public health organisation in the UK

Paul, German, based in Southern Europe, member of the Executive Team of a Scandinavian company in Engineering

Philip, Australian, Director of Procurement based in Thailand and working for a global German automotive company

Rose, Romanian, Manager Legal Affairs based in Italy, works for a British global company in the medical equipment sector

Sarah, Middle Eastern, HR Manager living in the UK, works for a pharmaceutical company with Headquarters in the USA

Steve, American, based in the USA, member of the Executive Team of a global company in engineering

Susan, Chinese, based in China, Head of Manufacturing working for a global German company

Thomas, Swedish, Strategy Director working for a global Danish company in engineering

15.2 Research basis - Collaborative Inquiry with leaders

This appendix provides additional information to that shared in Chapter 4.

The process and the approach

Given the nature of the topic that I was inquiring into (my assumption was that my co-researchers would have to share sensitive and personal stories), I developed a project contract in which I specified the purpose, scope, process and duration, as well as the research methodology that I would apply. The document also specified clearly my confidentiality agreement (including that of the people supporting me in the research, i.e., the Black Gazelle team and my supervisor), as well as their confidentiality agreement towards the overall research project and the further co-researchers. The 'contract' was then discussed at the beginning of the interview, signed and counter-signed at the end of the interview.

I was particularly thorough and careful when building the inquiry groups: I brought together only 'co-researchers' from different companies, with no potential competition and no supplier-client relationships between the companies. In all cases, the co-researchers had never met face-to-face. I personally had met six of them face-to-face several years before the research in the context of various training and consulting activities. As to the others, I had never met them face-to-face and had worked with them in some cases for over ten years, in other cases for less than one year.

Another conscious choice made was that I would not record anything, neither the interviews nor the Collaborative Inquiry sessions. Here again, I felt that I had to demonstrate to my co-researchers that they were maintaining their power over their own findings and learning. Anything recorded is an inherent part of a person's biography and the fact that people can distribute the recording (especially on such a sensitive topic) did not feel at all appropriate to me. Instead, I designed a process where co-researchers could maintain a significant amount of control over the results: for example, the stories shared during the interviews were anonymised and written up as Critical Incidents, which were then displayed on the (very secure) Black Gazelle Virtual Meeting Space for the interviewees (or co-researchers) to revalidate. The results of the inquiry sessions in small groups were displayed simultaneously during the sessions so that each session attendee could check at any time what was being documented and how.

As illustrated by the graphic in Chapter 4, each session (of 1.5 hours duration each) had a specific purpose and aim. Session one was to revalidate the Critical Incidents gathered from the ten interviews. For example, in wave one, there were over forty Critical Incidents that I had written up from my notes and displayed on the asynchronous platform. All ten managers had access to all Critical Incidents, although they were divided into three groups and could see only the comments of the people with whom they were in the same group. I decided to go for small groups because I was working with people from many different organisations (public and corporate) from my network. Given the sensitivity of the topic and the fact that these people did not know each other before (neither from the face-to-face, nor virtually) my assumption was that it would be easier for them to develop trust with each other if they were in a small group. I decided to use my cognitive knowledge of them as well as my intuition to form the groups, checking 'who might work well with whom'. I suggested the group constellation and asked each member of each group to let me know whether they agreed to work with the people that I was suggesting. At this point, I was very aware of my own 'power-to' decide on who should work with whom and I consciously decided to mitigate it by asking people to revalidate my suggestion. These were all accepted apart from one, even though in two cases they were carefully considered by the managers in question.

In wave two, we had twenty Critical Incidents. The members had access to all twenty Critical Incidents, although they were divided into two groups and could see only the comments of the people in their own group. The procedure with the second wave was the same as with wave one, apart from the difference mentioned in Chapter 4, namely that during the second session with the groups of the second wave I shared the emerging themes from wave one. This was in the spirit of truly sharing what was emerging in a collaborative way, as opposed to keeping the emerging themes from wave one to myself. This would have put me in a different place in terms of awareness and knowledge, as well as establishing a power differential that I was keen to avoid. So doing, I nevertheless had a dilemma, which was how to share the emerging themes from wave one without influencing too much the process that the two groups of wave two were going through for themselves. I was transparent with them about that.

I now provide below more details about the actual Collaborative Inquiry process.

Session 1: Revalidating and deepening the Critical Incidents

As mentioned in Chapter 4, I was particularly keen not to guide the co-researchers too strongly in their exploration of the concept of power and in the themes that they wished to focus on during the inquiry process. Before the first session, I invited the co-researchers to read the Critical Incidents displayed on the Black Gazelle Meeting Space platform with exclusive and secure access for each of the inquiry groups separately, to follow their interest and curiosity and to comment on the Critical Incidents that resonated most strongly with them. During the session, they were then prepared to expand more on why certain Critical Incidents in particular resonated the most with them. The further participants in the session would inquire into the explanations of their peers and add their comments. Very soon, relatively clear streams of themes were emerging. As each group was working on the same platform, but independently of each other (i.e., Group A could not see which themes were emerging in Group B, etc.), it was interesting to observe which of the themes seemed to be catching the attention of several groups and which seemed to be particularly relevant to one group. Here again, I was conscious of not wanting to guide the inquiry too much. My focus was more on the process itself: making sure that each step happened in a clear way and facilitating the group's reflection. Having said that, between the second and third sessions, I did share on the platform the themes that were emerging in the other groups. For example, I shared the themes emerging in Group A with Group C and vice versa, because they were asking about that and, as mentioned above, I did not want to keep the emerging knowledge to myself.

Session 2: Exploring the emerging themes

At the end of session one we had, as mentioned, relatively clear emerging themes. I posted them on the platform and asked the co-researchers to comment further on the themes. This meant leaving the Critical Incidents behind but not forgetting them, since they were the concretisation and the very basis of the themes themselves. I had to prompt the groups, but they did post their comments and questions regarding the themes that were resonating most strongly with them. In preparation for session two, I asked them to select one of the emerging themes and to be ready to comment on it: why was the theme particularly relevant to them? How did it manifest itself in their virtual leadership practice? During the second session, participants in turn commented on the emerging theme of their choice. The interesting thing was that they were also adding further Critical Incidents to the theme in question as a way to illustrate how relevant the theme was for them. I was particularly happy about that, because this enabled us to keep moving backwards and forwards between Critical Incidents and emerging themes. My aim was to keep doing so during the whole research process, as this was clearly enabling us to maintain the granularity of the themes, which could otherwise have become too abstract and thereby lost their meaning.

Then followed a process of in-depth reflection, looking at the common strands as well as the specific aspects emerging, and revalidating these between sessions two and three in the individual leadership practice in the context of the research members' roles and responsibilities.

At this stage, I also want to underline that the work in between the inquiry sessions was at least as important as that performed during the sessions. In this asynchronous work (between the sessions), each member of a given inquiry group would log on to our Black Gazelle Meeting Space and share their further reflections as well as further experiments in their ongoing virtual leadership practice. This was invaluable to deepen the insights, fine-tune the emerging themes and sharpen the research findings.

Session 3: Moving from emerging themes to emerging propositions

Another critical step in the process for me was how to come from the emerging themes to the emerging propositions. My original idea was to invite the group members at the end of session two to decide on the one theme that they would like to experiment with (in Action Inquiry fashion). This would be so that they could test in a more focused and detailed way the different aspects related to the theme in question on the basis of their own virtual leadership practice. As I raised the question at the end of the session with three of the groups, asking them to select one of the themes, they all pushed back, saying that they would find it difficult and limiting to focus on only one of the themes and that they would prefer to keep exploring all key themes emerging in the group in question. I could feel in the moment that they really wanted to keep full ownership of the research process and decided to go with that. The agreement that I had with them was therefore that they would experiment with the themes mentioned above and share their learning at the third session, so that the latter could be turned into some emerging propositions. Two groups preferred to select one specific theme though (hence stuck to my original plan) and to focus on it for their further research between sessions two and three.

During the third session, my co-researchers came back with their learning based on the specific selected themes; most of them had already been posting them on the asynchronous Black Gazelle Meeting Space. We went systematically from one co-researcher's learning to the others', documented the shared findings and analysed them further so that they could eventually be turned into propositions.

15.3 Focus exercise

You can find a recorded **focus exercise** (free of cost) on the website below:

https://www.black-gazelle.com/index.php?option=com_content &view=article&id=54&Itemid=266 (or go to https://www.black-gazelle.com/ then click on the TRAINING ON DEMAND tab, and scroll down).

15.4 Collaboration platforms and the use of cameras

Here are some more technical details regarding selected collaboration platforms and the use of cameras. Please note that this data is based on analysis carried out in March 2022. Things might change as collaboration platforms get updated on a regular basis.

When you share a document in the meeting, the number of people that can be seen at once on the screen is as follows:

- **MS Teams**: Max 9 people show in a 'ribbon' at the bottom of the shared content. < > will appear at the side of the gallery when there are more than 9 participants.

- **ZOOM**: Max 10 people can be seen if you enable 'gallery grid view'. < > will appear at the bottom of the gallery when there are more than 10 participants.

- **WebEx**: Max 6 people show in a 'ribbon' at the top of the shared content when using 'stack view'. < > will appear at the side of the gallery when there are more than 6 participants.

- **Adobe Connect:** Max 6 people show in a 'ribbon' at the bottom of the shared content. < > will appear at the side of the gallery when there are more than 6 participants.

If you do not share any documents, then the number of people that can be seen at once on the screen is much higher:

- **MS Teams**: 49 is the maximum that you can see on screen at one time. In "Large Gallery" view, navigation controls < > will appear at the bottom of the gallery when there are more than 49 participants. Participants use these navigation controls to view more video participants.

- **ZOOM**: Depending on your computer resolution and CPU speed, the desktop client can display up to 25 or 49 participants in a single screen of the 'Gallery' view. Navigation controls < > will appear at the side of the gallery when there are more than 49 participants.

- **WebEx:** Grid view allows you to see up to 25 participants at the same time. Navigation controls < > will appear at the side of the gallery when there are more than 25 participants.

- **Adobe Connect**: If the video pod is the primary view, this allows you to see up to 25 participants at the same time. Navigation controls < > will appear at the bottom of the gallery when there are more than 25 participants.

CHAPTER 16 –
Glossary

Action Research
Action Research is an approach to generating knowledge that combines different methods (such as reflection in groups, focus groups, interviews, personal reflection for example in the form of a journal). It is an interactive process combining the action with the reflection on this action. The assumption underlying this approach is that there is no learning (and knowledge) without action and that every action (if one takes the time to reflect on it) generates learning, and hence knowledge.

Action Research challenges traditional social science in the sense that it positions the generation of knowledge not as produced by experts who research, reflect on the knowledge available, express some hypothesis and test it with sampling actions – but as a process of active moment-to-moment theorising, data collecting, and inquiry occurring in the midst of emergent structures. The knowledge is gained through action and for action.

For example, Reason and Bradbury (2001) advocate that Action Research is about helping organisations and individuals to develop more practical knowledge and well-being (economic, political, psychological and spiritual): they consider the purpose of Action Research as: "[...] to produce practical knowledge that is useful to people in the everyday conduct of their lives." (Idem, p. 2)

McKernan (1996) shares this point of view: for him "The aim of Action Research, as opposed to much traditional or fundamental research, is to solve the immediate and pressing day-to-day problems of practitioners." (Idem, p. 3).

Asynchronous mode of working

See also 'synchronous mode of working'

Asynchronous work in the virtual space means that all people work in their own time (at a different time) and usually from different locations.

Examples of asynchronous work include:

- participating in a word-based online conference. All log on to a virtual platform where they can exchange written messages and join the debate in their own time. For example, from a UK-based time perspective it might be that one person logs in at 10.00 am, another at 7.00 pm, another at 11.00 pm, etc.; the conference and the exchange of views takes place but is stretched over a certain number of days.

- participating in a blog (all log in at the time they want but participate in the same conversation)

- Emails also represent a form of asynchronous work.

Collaborative Inquiry

Also known as 'Cooperative Inquiry', it belongs to the same category of research approach as Action Research. It was first proposed by Heron (1988) and later expanded by Reason and Bradbury (2001).

Collaborative Inquiry particularly underlines the fact that, to be valid, research in social science needs to happen 'with' rather than 'on' people. It emphasises that all active participants are fully involved in research decisions and therefore all participants to the research become "co-researchers".

Cooperative Inquiry creates a research cycle with four different types of knowledge: propositional knowing (the claims of knowledge and statements that we make based on the outcomes of our research), practical knowing (the knowledge that comes with actually doing what you propose), experiential knowing (the knowledge we receive in the actual moment of the interaction with our environment) and presentational knowing (the ways we choose to express and convey the knowledge that we have generated through our actions, in other words the way we choose to document our practice).

Extravert or Introvert
The concepts of Extraversion and Introversion each represent one of the four dimensions in the Myers Briggs Type Indicator, developed by Briggs and Briggs Myers, based on Jung's theory.

This dimension looks at whether a person has a preference for the outer or inner world. A person with an Extravert Preference draws energy from people and things around themselves as opposed to a person with an Introvert Preference who draws energy from within themselves, ideas and concepts. For example, a person with an Extravert Preference learns from experience and discussion with others; a person with an Introvert Preference learns from reading or understanding and privileges reflection on their own.

Introjection (see also projection)
Introjection is a concept rooted in psychoanalysis. An introjection is an unconscious process, by which a person makes ways of thinking, behaviours or feelings of another person, their own.

Process awareness
Managers who are process aware pay attention not only to the work on the agenda (content discussions, analysis of data and problems, decision-making), but also to the team dynamics and the process of relating and working together between the team members. For example, they notice who remains silent, who keeps repeating the same things, whether the team diverges from the agenda, etc.

Projection (see also introjection)
Projection is a concept rooted in psychoanalysis. When a person is projecting, they unconsciously attribute to other people the way they feel or think at a given moment. For example, a person is very angry and thinks that the other people attending the meeting are angry and do not realise that this feeling of anger is only their own feeling that they do not own. Projections happen more often in the virtual space than in a face-to-face environment.

Self-awareness
Managers who are self-aware are not only reflective but also reflexive.

Reflective/reflexive

Reflection is understood to be a cognitive or intellectual activity, consisting of thinking about something in an objective, logical and neutral way, based on a realistic view of the world with a reality to be discovered, measured, categorised and properly explained.

Reflexivity on the other hand, is based on a social constructionist view of the world; in other words, there is no one single reality of the world – we shape our own social and organisational realities. Cunliffe (2009, p.11) explains: "[...] reflexivity goes deeper than reflection, because it means interrogating the taken-for-granted by questioning our relationship with our social world and the ways in which we account for our experience. [...] Managers as reflexive practitioners believe that we shape our social and organisational realities between us in our everyday interactions, and routinely engage in questioning this process."

A **self-reflexive** manager explores on a regular basis how (s)he IS in the world (as opposed to what (s)he does), how (s)he experiences and constructs their own identity/ies, the ones of others, their organisation and the world in general. (S)he also notices their own emotional reactions for example to what is being said in a meeting. This is particularly important to strengthen their own 'power-to'.

Synchronous mode of working

See also 'asynchronous mode of working'.

Synchronous work in the virtual space means that all people are working at the same time, albeit from different geographical places.

Examples of synchronous work include:

- having a teleconference with several people based in different locations

- having a virtual meeting (web-based) with several people based in different locations

- having a video conference with several people located in different places

- having a virtual (web-based) workshop with several people located in different places.

Traditional leading/working
In the context of my book, I use 'traditional leadership' to mean any leadership that occurs largely in the face-to-face mode, though clearly this does not exclude all phone calls, emails etc.

REFERENCES

Benfari, R.C., Wilkinson, H.E. and Orth, C.D. (1986) "The effective use of power" *Business Horizons*, 29, pp. 12–16

Bion, W.R. (1961) *Experiences in Groups and Other Papers.* Taylor and Francis e-Library

Buchanan, D. and Badham, R. (2010) *Power, Politics and Organizational Change.* 2nd Ed. London: Sage

Caulat, Gh. (2012) *Virtual Leadership – Learning to lead differently.* Faringdon: Libri Publishing

Chen, S., Lee-Chai, A.Y. and Bargh, J.A. (2001) "Relationship orientation as a moderator of the effects of social power" *Journal of Personality and Social Psychology*, 80(2), pp. 137–187

Contreras, F., Bayka, E. and Abid, G. (2020) "E-Leadership and Teleworking in Times of Covid-19 and Beyond: What we know and Where do we go" *Frontiers in Psychology*, 11, Article 590271, pp. 1–11.

Cunliffe, A.L. (2009) "The Philosopher Leader: On Relationism, Ethics and Reflexivity. A Critical Perspective to Teaching Leadership" *Management Learning*, 40(87)

Eagly, A.H. (2007) "Female leadership advantage and disadvantage: resolving the contradictions" *Psychology of Women Quarterly* 31, pp. 1–12

Eagly, A.H. and Karau S. (2002) "Role Congruity Theory of prejudice toward female leaders" *Psychological Review* 109, pp. 573–598

Flanagan, J.C. (1954) "The Critical Incident Technique" *Psychological Bulletin*, 51(4)

Foulkes, S.H. (1948) *Introduction to Group Analytic Psychotherapy.* London: Karnac

French, J.R.P. and Raven, B. (1958) "The bases of social power" in D. Cartwright (ed.), *Studies in Social Power.* Ann Arbor, MI: Institute for Social Research

Galinsky, A.D., Gruenfeld, D.H and Magee, J.C. (2003) "From Power to Action" *Journal of Personality and Social Psychology*, 85(3), pp. 453–466

Gibbs, J.L., Gibson, C. B., Grushina, S.V. and Dunlop, P.D. (2021) "Understanding orientations to participation: overcoming status differences to foster engagement in global teams" in *European Journal of Work and Organizational Psychology*, pp. 1–19.

Hofstede, G see http://www.geert-hofstede.com

Jarvenpaa, S.L. and Keating, E. (2021) "When do good communication models fail in global virtual teams?" *Organizational Dynamics* 50, pp. 1–12

Klaas, B.S., Olson-Buchanan, J.B. and Ward, A-K. (2012) "The Determinants of Alternative Forms of Workplace Voice: An Integrative Perspective" *Journal of Management*, 38(1), pp. 314–345.

Leighton, J. (2021) "Stanford researchers identify four causes for 'Zoom fatigue' and their simple fixes" *Stanford News* (htttps:// news.standford. edu/2021/02/23/four-causes-zoom-fatigue-solutions/)

Magee, J.C. (2008) "Social Hierarchy: The Self-Reinforcing Nature of Power and Status" *The Academy of Management Annals*, 2(1), pp. 351–398.

Marschan, R., Welch, D. and Welch, L. (1997) "Language: The forgotten factor in multinational management" *European Management Journal*, 15(5), pp. 591–598

McKernan, J. (1996) *Curriculum Action Research.* 2nd Edition, Kogan Page.

Melé, Domènec and Rosanas, Josep M. (2003) "Power, Freedom and Authority in Management: Mary Parker Follett's 'PowerWith'" *Philosophy of Management* 3(2), pp. 35–46

Méndez García, M.D.C. and Pérez Cañado, M.L. (2005) "Language and Power: Raising Awareness of the Role of Language in Multicultural Teams" *Language and Intercultural Communication*, 5(1), pp. 86–104.

Myers Briggs Type Indicator Foundation http://www.myersbriggs.org./ my-mbti-personality-type/mbti-basics/

Nurmi, N., Bosch-Sijtsema, P., Sivunen, A. and Fruchter, R. (2009) "Who Shouts Louder: Power Dynamics in Virtual Teams" article published in *proceedings of IWIC* – 2009, February 20–21, Palo Alto, California ACM, pp.1–9

Pansardi, P. and Bindi, M. (2021) "The new concepts of power? Power over, power-to and power-with" *Journal of Political Power*, 14(1), pp. 51–71

Panteli, N. and Fineman, S. (2006) "The sound of Silence: the case of virtual team organizing" in *Behaviour and Information Technology*, 24(5), pp. 347–352

Panteli, N. and Tucker, R. (2009) "Power and Trust in Global Virtual Teams" *Communication of the ACM*, December 2009, 52(12), pp. 1–3

Pfeffer, J. (2010) *Power: Why some people have it – and others don't.* New York: HarperCollins

Reason, P. and Bradbury, H. (2001) "Introduction: Inquiry and Participation in Search of a World Worthy of Human Aspiration" in Reason, P. and Bradbury, H. (eds) *Handbook of Action Research*. pp. 1–14, London: Sage

Reitz, M. and Higgins, J. (2019) *Speak Up – Say what needs to be said and hear what needs to be heard*. Harlow: Pearson.

Russel, B. (1938) *A New Social Analysis*. London: George Allen & Unwin

Tavenner, Jr. F. (2019) *Supervisors' Dyadic Relationship with Remote Workers Compared with traditional Co-located Workers: A Case Study*, A Dissertation submitted to the Faculty of the Graduate School of Education and Human Development of the George Washington University in partial fulfilment of the requirements for the degree of Doctor of Education.

Tom Tong, S. and Walther, J.B. (2015) "The Confirmation and Disconfirmation of Expectancies" *Computer-Mediated Communication in Communication Research*, 42(2), pp. 186–212

Weinberg, H. (2014) *The Paradox of Internet Groups. Alone in the Presence of Virtual Others*. London: Karnac

Yong-Kwan Lim, J., Chidambaram L. and Carte T. (2008) "Impression management and leadership emergence in Virtual Settings: The Role of Gender and Media" in *Proceedings of JAIS Theory Development Workshop*. Sprouts: Working Papers on Information Systems, 8(22), pp. 1–28